BASIC KEYBOARD SKILLS

BASIC

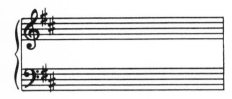

KEYBOARD

SKILLS

AN INTRODUCTION TO ACCOMPANIMENT IMPROVISATION, TRANSPOSITION
AND MODULATION, WITH AN APPENDIX ON SIGHT READING

WILLIAM PELZ

Butler University

GREENWOOD PRESS, PUBLISHERS
WESTPORT, CONNECTICUT

Library of Congress Cataloging in Publication Data

Pelz, William.
  Basic keyboard skills.

  Reprint of ed. published by Allyn and Bacon,
Boston.
  Includes index.
  1. Musical accompaniment. 2. Improvisation
(Music) 3. Harmony, Keyboard. 4. Sight-reading
(Music) I. Title.
[MT236.P36 1980]   786.3'041   80-22820
ISBN 0-313-22882-5 (lib. bdg.)

786.3
P

TO ROWENA

Reprinted with the permission of Allyn and Bacon, Inc.

Reprinted from an original copy in the collection of the
Library at the Evansville Campus, Indiana State University.

Reprinted in 1981 by Greenwood Press
A division of Congressional Information Service, Inc.
88 Post Road West, Westport, Connecticut 06881

Printed in the United States of America

10 9 8 7 6 5 4 3 2 1

INTRODUCTION

Basic Keyboard Skills IS A BOOK FOR THOSE WHO DESIRE TO DEVELOP the ability to improvise accompaniments, transpose, modulate and sight-read. It assumes that the reader has completed a year or two of piano study and has done (and will continue to do so, concurrently with the use of this book) work in basic theory and harmony. It is concerned with the application of fundamental ideas in music theory to the following practical ends:

The teaching of rote songs at the piano;
The playing of accompaniments for singing games and folk dancing;
The accompanying of instrumental and vocal soloists and ensembles in the studio, rehearsal room and concert hall;
The accompanying of group singing on social occasions, and
Church service playing.

The concepts and problems involved in these disciplines are presented briefly and directly. Each concept is illustrated by means of musical examples. Exercise materials at the end of each chapter embrace all the commonly-used keys, meters and tempi, and appear in problem forms directly applicable to the practical situations listed above.

While accompaniment improvisation, transposition, modulation and sight reading are indispensable skills for the keyboard performer in particular, there are in addition many instances in which they can be of valuable assistance to the conductor, the critic and the music history student.

William Pelz

CONTENTS

CONTENTS   vii

BASIC KEYBOARD SKILLS

PART ONE

ACCOMPANIMENT
IMPROVISATION

CHAPTER ONE

Accompaniments Using the Principal Chords of Major Keys in Block Style

KEYBOARD ACCOMPANIMENTS TO CHILDREN'S SONGS, FOLK SONGS AND simple dance music should provide two musical elements—harmonic support and rhythmic movement. An accompaniment that also carries the melody is most useful. The playing of accompaniments, in common with other types of instrumental performance, requires the ability to play accurately, musically and in tempo. Competence in the contriving and performance of accompaniments is thus a complex resolving into three constituents:

(a) the determination of the harmony appropriate to a given melody;
(b) the selection of a suitable rhythmic background;
(c) drill in the performance of selected accompaniment patterns in all the practical keys.

Many simple melodies strongly suggest the harmonies appropriate for their accompaniments. This results from the fact that such tunes are constructed almost exclusively from notes belonging to the principal chords of a key (I, IV, V₇). When non-harmonic tones are present in a folkish tune, they are few and can be easily recognized.

EXAMPLE 1. ENGLISH FOLK SONG IN THE KEY OF G MAJOR.

Traditional

A comparison of the English Folk Melody in Example 1 with the principal chords of the key of G major:

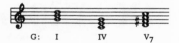

reveals that considerable variety in harmonization is possible within the limited framework of the three principal chords. Every melody note is a member of one or more of the principal chords in the key of G major. In instances where a note is a member of more than one of the principal chords, alternate harmonizations of that note are possible, as shown by the three optional harmonizations in Example 1. The two determining factors in chord choice are:

(a) strong tonal progression

The progressions among the three principal chords of a key that reinforce key feeling are as follows:

$$I\text{-}V_7$$
$$I\text{-}IV$$
$$V_7\text{-}I$$
$$IV\text{-}I$$
$$IV\text{-}V_7$$

V₇-IV is not a strong tonal progression, and should not be used in music of the type being treated here. For example, the note D in measure 4 of Example 1, although a member of the V₇ chord in the key of G, cannot be harmonized with V₇ since the following melody note (E) must be harmonized with IV, and the result would be the weak tonal progression V₇-IV.

(b) traditional cadence structure

Folk music, popular songs, dance music and children's music are usually constructed in four-measure or eight-measure phrases, and each phrase ends with a cadence. The final cadence is almost invariably authentic (V₇-I). Intermediate cadences may be authentic, but also may be half-cadences (I-V₇; IV-V₇). On rare occasions the plagal cadence (IV-I) will be used either as an intermediate cadence or as a final cadence. The English Folk Song of Example 1 is constructed of two eight-measure phrases; there is a half-cadence at the close of the first phrase and an authentic cadence closing the final phrase. Note that this cadence relationship holds for all three optional harmonizations given in Example 1.

For the practical purpose of keeping the accompaniment chords in positions from which it is easy to progress from one to another on the keyboard, the I, IV and V₇ chords are played as follows in the key of G major:

EXAMPLE 2. THE PRINCIPAL CHORDS OF G MAJOR IN PRACTICAL PLAYING POSITIONS.

Note that in the practical playing position of the V₇ chord shown above, the fifth of the chord (the second degree of the scale) has been omitted in order to maintain consistently three parts in the accompaniment. It should be remembered, however, that the V₇ chord is available and appropriate for harmonizing the second degree of the scale when it appears as a note in a melody. (See the penultimate melody note of Example 3 below, and note its harmonization with V₇).

ACCOMPANIMENT IMPROVISATION   5

EXAMPLE 3. ENGLISH FOLK TUNE HARMONIZED WITH BLOCK CHORD ACCOMPANIMENT, USING PRACTICAL PLAYING POSITIONS OF THE CHORDS SHOWN IN OPTION 1 OF EXAMPLE 1.

(Note that in measures 1 and 9 of the above example, the top note (D) of the left-hand chord is omitted, since it would interfere with the playing of the melody, which includes the note D in both these measures.)

EXAMPLE 4. ENGLISH FOLK TUNE HARMONIZED WITH BLOCK CHORD ACCOMPANIMENT, USING PRACTICAL PLAYING POSITIONS OF THE CHORDS SHOWN IN OPTION 3 OF EXAMPLE 1.

In this harmonization, the note B in measure 7 is considered a non-harmonic tone (in this instance a passing tone) and is not harmonized.

On the second beats of measures 1 and 9 of the above example, the top note of the left-hand V₇ chord is omitted since it would interfere with the playing of the melody, which includes the note D in both these places.

When the third of V₇ (the leading tone of the key) appears in the melody on an accented beat, or precedes the tonic note in the melody at a cadence, the following form of V₇ is used in the left hand to avoid the acoustically undesirable doubled third in the V₇ chord, and to avoid a progression in parallel octaves between the melody and the bass:

$$V_7(^4_3)$$

EXAMPLE 4(A). THE USE OF V₇ WITH THE LEADING TONE (ACCENTED) IN THE MELODY.

God Give Ye Merry Christmastide
Old English Carol

(1) Third of V₇ (leading tone of key) in melody at cadence.

EXAMPLE 4(B). THE USE OF V₇ WITH THE LEADING TONE (UNACCENTED) IN THE MELODY.

Carry Me Back to Old Virginny
James A. Bland

(1) Third of V₇ (leading tone of key) progressing to tonic note in cadence. (In this case, the leading tone is preceded by an accented passing note or *appoggiatura by step*.)

ASSIGNMENT NO. 1

Harmonize the following tunes with block chords in the style illustrated in Examples 3 and 4. Use only I, IV and V7. Non-harmonic tones (passing notes, neighboring or auxiliary tones, suspensions, appoggiaturas, échappées) and up-beats are marked (*) and should not be harmonized. Use only the strong tonal progressions listed in Chapter 1. When the melody descends low enough to double a tone in the left-hand accompaniment, omit that tone from the accompaniment.

Note: The melodies in this assignment are suitable for use with the accompaniment chords given in the registers shown immediately preceding each tune. In later chapters, and elsewhere, the student will occasionally encounter melodies—particularly in the keys of Bb, Ab and A—whose low range will necessitate playing the accompaniment chords an octave lower than given in the exercise section of this chapter, to avoid interference with the right-hand melody.

Principal chords of C major:

1. *Brightly*   Austrian Folk Tune

Principal chords of G major:

2. *Gaily*   *Humpty Dumpty*
Nursery Tune

Principal chords of F major:

I   IV   V₇   V₇

3. *Moderato*

Ding Dong Bell
Nursery Tune

F: I   V₇   I   I   V₇   I   IV   I   V₇ V₇   I

Principal chords of D major:

I   IV   V₇   V₇

4. *Allegretto*

German Folk Tune

D: I   I   IV   I   I   I   V₇   V₇   I

Principal chords of Bb major:

I   IV   V₇   V₇

5. *Tenderly*

Away in a Manger
Martin Luther

Bb: I   V₇

I   IV   V₇

(1) Added 6th to the IV chord. The interval of the 6th above the root of the IV chord (2nd degree of the scale) is often harmonized with IV.

Principal chords of A major:

I IV V₇ V₇

6. *Moderato*   *Lavender's Blue*
                          Old English

Principal chords of E♭ major:

I IV V₇ V₇

7. *Con spirito*   *Hickory Dickory Dock*
                          Nursery Tune

Principal chords of E major:

I IV V₇ V₇

8. *Moderato*   *Little Miss Muffet*
                          Nursery Tune

Principal chords of A♭ major:

I   IV   V₇   V₇

9. *Allegretto*

Mary Had a Little Lamb
Nursery Tune

CHAPTER TWO

Accompaniments Using Simple Figurations of the Principal Chords in Major Keys

THE BLOCK CHORD ACCOMPANIMENTS PRESENTED IN CHAPTER 1 EX-
hibit adequate harmonic support and a modicum of rhythmic movement.
Added rhythmic and textural interest can be imparted to the accompaniment by figuring the left-hand chords. The following figurations show
two of the many possibilities for achieving a degree of rhythmic move-
ment in each of the four common meters ($\frac{4}{4}$, $\frac{3}{4}$, $\frac{2}{4}$, $\frac{6}{8}$). Each figuration is
applied to the principal chords in the key of C major.

EXAMPLE 5(A). LEFT-HAND FIGURATION FOR $\frac{4}{4}$ METER.

EXAMPLE 5(B). LEFT-HAND FIGURATION FOR $\frac{4}{4}$ METER.

I   IV V_7 V_7

EXAMPLE 6(A). LEFT-HAND FIGURATION FOR $\frac{3}{4}$ METER.

I   IV V_7 V_7

EXAMPLE 6(B). LEFT-HAND FIGURATION FOR $\frac{3}{4}$ METER.

I   IV V_7 V_7

EXAMPLE 7(A). LEFT-HAND FIGURATION FOR $\frac{2}{4}$ METER.

I   IV V_7 V_7

EXAMPLE 7(B). LEFT-HAND FIGURATION FOR $\frac{2}{4}$ METER.

I   IV V_7 V_7

EXAMPLE 8(A). LEFT-HAND FIGURATION FOR $\frac{6}{8}$ METER.

I   IV V_7 V_7

EXAMPLE 8(B). LEFT-HAND FIGURATION FOR $\frac{6}{8}$ METER.

I   IV V_7 V_7

Note: The ¾ figurations shown in Examples 6(a) and 6(b) can be adapted to ⅜ meter as follows:

When using a figured accompaniment, do not continue the figuration through the last measure of the song. The relaxation of rhythmic movement typical of the closing cadence requires a block chord on the final I.

EXAMPLE 9. THE LAST FOUR MEASURES OF EXAMPLE 1, USING THE FIGURATION GIVEN IN EXAMPLE 7(A), AND CLOSING WITH A BLOCK CHORD ON THE FINAL I.

EXAMPLE 10. THE LAST FOUR MEASURES OF EXAMPLE 1, USING THE FIGURATION GIVEN IN EXAMPLE 7(B), AND CLOSING WITH A BLOCK CHORD ON THE FINAL I.

In places within a phrase where the harmonic rhythm does not permit a full measure of the figuration pattern, employ either block chords or a modified (shortened) version of the figuration.

EXAMPLE 11. FIGURED ACCOMPANIMENT USING BLOCK CHORDS IN MEASURES WHERE THE HARMONIC RHYTHM DOES NOT PERMIT A FULL MEASURE OF THE FIGURATION PATTERN.

Hickory Dickory Dock
Nursery Tune

EXAMPLE 12. FIGURED ACCOMPANIMENT USING MODIFIED (SHORTENED) VERSION OF THE FIGURATION WHERE THE HARMONIC RHYTHM DOES NOT PERMIT A FULL MEASURE OF THE FIGURATION PATTERN.

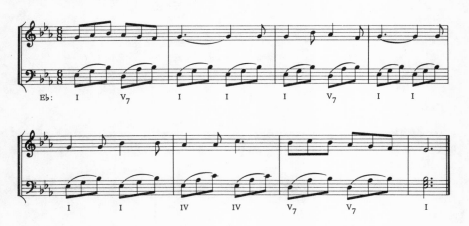

ASSIGNMENT NO. 2

Harmonize again the melodies in Assignment No. 1, Chapter 1, using the left-hand figuration patterns given in Examples 5, 6, 7 and 8 of Chapter 2.

CHAPTER THREE

Accompaniments Using Block Chords and Simple Figurations in Minor Keys

A PARTICULAR KEY SIGNATURE MAY INDICATE EITHER A MAJOR OR A minor key. In children's music, simple dance music and folk music the final melody note is almost invariably the keynote. Thus, a tune in the key of E♭ major will end on the note E♭, and one in the key of A major will close on the note A. The same is true of melodies in minor keys. A melody in D minor will end on the note D; one in C minor, on the note C. The following table shows the key signatures and closing notes of the major and minor keys in which simple song and dance music are most often written.

EXAMPLE 13. TABLE OF KEY SIGNATURES AND CLOSING NOTES OF THE COMMONLY-USED MAJOR AND MINOR KEYS.

Key Signature	If Closing Note Is	Key Is	If Closing Note Is	Key Is
		C major		A minor
		G major		E minor
		D major		B minor (rare)
		A major		F# minor (rare)
		E major		C# minor (rare)
		F major		D minor
		Bb major		G minor
		Eb major		C minor
		Ab major		F minor

EXAMPLE 14. THE PRINCIPAL CHORDS OF THE COMMONLY-USED MINOR KEYS (NOTE THAT THE V_7 CHORD IS THE SAME AS FOR MAJOR KEYS WITH THE SAME LETTER NAME).

ACCOMPANIMENT IMPROVISATION

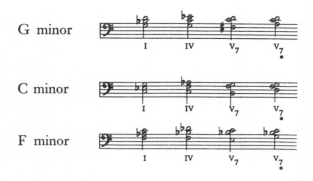

G minor — I IV V₇ V₇

C minor — I IV V₇ V₇

F minor — I IV V₇ V₇

ASSIGNMENT NO. 3

Harmonize the following melodies, using this procedure:

(a) Referring to Example 13, determine the major or minor key in which the tune is written;

(b) Using the principal chords of the determined key, harmonize in both block style and figured style. Chords for minor keys are given in Example 14; major key chords are given in the exercise section of Chapter 1.

1. *Andante* Spanish Folk Song

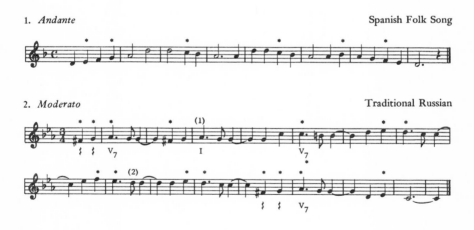

2. *Moderato* Traditional Russian

⁽¹⁾ The added 6th is frequently used as melody note with the I chord.
⁽²⁾ The added 6th to the IV chord (also quite frequent).

3. *Rollicking* *We Won't Go Home until Morning*
College Song

4. *Andante*

Go Down, Moses
Negro Spiritual

_____

(1) Added 6th to the IV chord.

5. *Tempo di valse*

My Nellie's Blue Eyes
American Folk Song

6. *Con moto*

Hungarian Dance
Johannes Brahms

7. *Allegretto*

Italian Folk Dance

8. *With spirit*

Polly Wolly Doodle
Traditional

9. *Slowly*   Russian Folk Song

CHAPTER FOUR

The V₇ of V in Block Chord and Figured Accompaniments

IT IS OFTEN POSSIBLE AND MUSICALLY DESIRABLE TO PRECEDE THE dominant chord at either the half cadence or the final cadence with the V₇ of V (the dominant of the dominant). The use of this progression injects a degree of chromaticism into the predominantly diatonic harmony characteristic of simple music, adding a welcome touch of color. Following, in Example 15, are the V₇ of V chords (symbolized V_7/V) of the commonly used keys. Note that this chord is the same for both major and minor keys bearing the same letter name. It always precedes V₇ of the key, and may follow either I or IV of the key.

EXAMPLE 15. THE V_7/V CHORDS OF THE COMMONLY USED KEYS (MAJOR AND MINOR).

C	G	F	D	B♭	A	E♭	E	A♭

In practical playing positions:

$v_7/V\ (v_2^4/V)$ ————————————————————————

V_7 of V chords are subject to the same figurations shown for the principal chords in Chapter 2. Note that, as in V_7 of the key, the fifth of V_7/V is omitted in practical playing position. Remember, however, that the fifth of this chord (the sixth degree of the scale) is frequently harmonized with V_7/V.

EXAMPLE 16. THE V_7 OF V PRECEDING V_7 OF THE KEY AT THE HALF CADENCE.

My Bonnie
Traditional

(1) The added 6th to the IV chord.
(2) Note modification of the accompaniment figuration necessitated by the descent of the melody into the accompaniment range.

EXAMPLE 17. THE V_7 OF V PRECEDING V_7 OF THE KEY AT THE FINAL CADENCE.

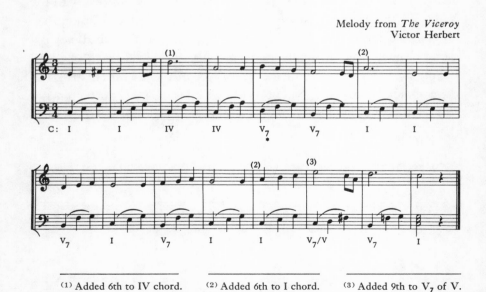

Melody from *The Viceroy*
Victor Herbert

(1) Added 6th to IV chord.   (2) Added 6th to I chord.   (3) Added 9th to V_7 of V.

ASSIGNMENT NO. 4

Harmonize the following melodies using this procedure:

(1) Determine the modality (major or minor) of the melody (see Example 13).
(2) Select the chords appropriate to the determined key. See Assignment No. 1, Chapter 1, for major key chords; see Example 14 for minor key chords; see Example 15 for V₇/V chords.
(3) Note the meter and harmonize with an appropriate figuration in the accompaniment. See Examples 5, 6, 7 and 8 for figurations of the principal chords (also applicable to V₇/V chords).
(4) Beginning with this assignment, the identification of upbeats, non-harmonic tones, added 6ths and alternate positions of V₇ will be the responsibility of the student.
(5) As in preceding exercises, the harmonic rhythm of particular tunes will occasionally necessitate the modification of the figuration patterns given in Examples 5, 6, 7 and 8.

1. *Molto moderato*

Slumber Song
Franz Schubert

2. *Moderato*

Cowboy's Lament
American Folk Song

3. *Con moto*

Russian Folk Song

4. *Moderato*

Home on the Range
American Folk Song

5. *Andante*

Slumber Song
Robert Schumann

6. *Con moto*

Swanee River
Stephen Collins Foster

---

(1) The 9th of V_7 of V.
(2) V_7 of V (block chord).
(3) V_7 (block chord).

7. *Allegretto*

Old French Song
Peter Ilyitch Tschaikowsky

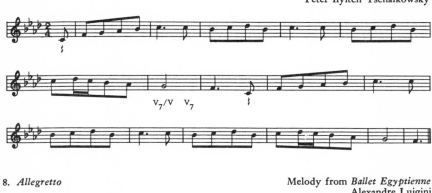

8. *Allegretto*

Melody from *Ballet Egyptienne*
Alexandre Luigini

9. *Moderato*

Gavotte
Ethelbert Nevin

(1) Added 6th to V_7.

10. *Allegretto*

Chiapanecas
Mexican Folk Song

11. *Scherzando*

La Zingara
Carl Bohm

12. *Vivo*

Mazurka
Léo Delibes

13. *Moderato*

Fragment from *The Little Duchess*
Reginald De Koven

14. *Allegro*

Waltz from *Faust* (fragment)
Charles Gounod

15. *Fast*

Italian Folk Melody

etc.

CHAPTER FIVE

The V₇ of IV in Block Chord and Figured Accompaniments

ANOTHER CHROMATIC CHORD USEFUL FOR ADDING COLOR TO THE harmonization of simple music is the V₇ of IV (dominant of the subdominant). This chord usually follows I of the key, and always precedes IV of the key. Occasionally within a phrase (but not at the beginning or end) the V₇ of IV may substitute for I of the key, following V₇ of the key. As in the case of V₇ of V, the V₇ of IV is subject to the same figurations used for the principal chords of a key, and is the same for both major and minor keys bearing the same letter name. It is symbolized V₇/IV.

EXAMPLE 18. THE V₇ OF IV CHORDS OF THE COMMONLY USED KEYS (MAJOR AND MINOR).

In practical playing positions (block style):

EXAMPLE 19. THE V₇ OF IV FOLLOWING I OF THE KEY AND PRECEDING IV (THE FOLLOWING MELODY IS #1 OF ASSIGNMENT #1, WHICH HAS BEEN HARMONIZED PREVIOUSLY USING ONLY THE COMMON CHORDS [I, IV, V₇]. NOTE HOW THE USE OF V₇ OF IV ADDS TO THE HARMONIC INTEREST OF THE ACCOMPANIMENT).

Austrian Folk Tune

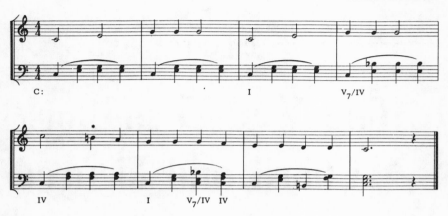

EXAMPLE 20. THE V₇ OF IV SUBSTITUTING FOR I OF THE KEY, FOLLOWING V₇ OF THE KEY AND PRECEDING IV. NOTE AGAIN HOW THE USE OF V₇ OF IV ADDS TO THE HARMONIC INTEREST.

Humpty Dumpty
Traditional

ASSIGNMENT NO. 5

Harmonize the following melodies, using the procedure prescribed in Assignment No. 4. Practical playing positions of the V₇ of IV chords are shown in Example 18 of this chapter. The melodies given below are in both major and minor keys. Each melody offers opportunities for using either V₇ of V or V₇ of IV (in most cases, both), as well as the common chords of the key.

1. *Lively*

Yankee Doodle
Traditional

* Accented passing note.

2. *Andante*

My Old Kentucky Home
Stephen Collins Foster

3. *Andantino*

Theme from *Mazurka*
Frédéric François Chopin

4. *Allegro*

Oh, Susannah
Stephen Collins Foster

5. *Lively*

Dixie
Daniel D. Emmett

*Added 9th to V_7 chord.

6. *Cantabile*

Theme from *Romance*
Peter Ilyitch Tschaikowsky

7. *Espressivo*

Carry Me Back to Old Virginny
James A. Bland

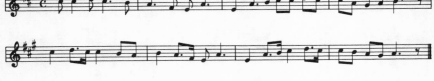

8. *Gaily*

Jingle Bells
J. Pierpont

ACCOMPANIMENT IMPROVISATION

9. *Briskly*

For He's a Jolly Good Fellow
Traditional

10. *Slowly*

Good Night, Ladies
Traditional College Song

11. *Moderato*

God Give Ye Merry Christmastide
Old English Carol

12. *With spirit*

Rio Grande
Sea Chanty

13. *A la valse*

Expectation
Traditional Russian Waltz

14. *Con brio*

Israeli Folk Song

ACCOMPANIMENT IMPROVISATION   33

16. *Allegro* Israeli Folk Song

CHAPTER SIX

Introductions

A SINGING GROUP WILL MAKE A GOOD INITIAL IMPRESSION ONLY IF there is agreement on tempo at the beginning of the song, and a confident attack on the first note. The accompanist, by providing the proper kind of introduction, holds a major responsibility for a good beginning, for he must adequately indicate to the singers both the tempo and the beginning note.

A common practice among church organists, in accompanying the singing of hymns, is to play the entire hymn through once before the congregation begins the first stanza. Not only does this acquaint the singers with what might possibly be an unfamiliar tune; it also establishes both the tempo of the hymn and, through the context of the tonality, its beginning note.

In situations involving the singing of familiar tunes it is not necessary to indicate the tempo, since this is known through tradition. Thus, for songs such as *America the Beautiful* and *Silent Night*, the only requirement is to indicate the beginning note. This can be done satisfactorily with a single chord whose top note is the beginning note for the singers.

EXAMPLE 21(A). A SINGLE CHORD USED AS AN INTRODUCTION, WITH THE FIRST MELODY NOTE IN THE TOP PART.

Katherine Lee Bates

America the Beautiful
Samuel A. Ward

EXAMPLE 21(B). A SINGLE CHORD, WITH THE FIRST MELODY NOTE IN THE TOP PART, USED AS AN INTRODUCTION.

Joseph Mohr

Silent Night
Franz Gruber

After an introduction of the single chord type it is necessary for the accompanist (unless a song leader or conductor is directing) to indicate by a nod or some other gesture the exact point at which singing is to begin.

In the singing of a new song (in which case the single chord introduction would not suffice), or in a program situation where the playing of the complete song as an introduction would unduly retard the pace of the performance, the most useful type of introduction consists of a phrase or two taken from the song to be performed. Such an introductory passage may consist of the first one or two phrases of the song, the last one or two, or the first and last phrases, depending on which arrangement most effectively indicates the beginning note.

EXAMPLE 22. THE FIRST PHRASE USED AS AN INTRODUCTION.

Plaintively

Careless Love
Southern Mountain Song

EXAMPLE 23. THE LAST PHRASE USED AS AN INTRODUCTION.

Con brio

Turkey in the Straw
American Square Dance Tune

ACCOMPANIMENT IMPROVISATION

EXAMPLE 24. THE FIRST AND LAST PHRASES USED AS AN INTRODUCTION.

Moderato

Red River Valley
Western Folk Song

The phrase-type introductions illustrated in Examples 22, 23 and 24 are usually the most suitable for music used in dancing and other types of action.

ASSIGNMENT NO. 6

Play, with varied figured accompaniments, the exercises of Assignment No. 5, Chapter 5. Precede each exercise with the type(s) of introduction indicated below:

(1) *Yankee Doodle:* (a) single chord; (b) last phrase.
(2) *My Old Kentucky Home:* (a) single chord; (b) first and last phrase.
(3) Theme from *Mazurka:* last two phrases.
(4) *Oh, Susannah:* last phrase.
(5) *Dixie:* last phrase.
(6) Theme from *Romance:* first two phrases (entire excerpt).
(7) *Carry Me Back to Old Virginny:* (a) single chord; (b) first and last phrases.

(8) *Jingle Bells:* (a) single chord; (b) last two phrases.
(9) *For He's a Jolly Good Fellow:* last two phrases.
(10) *Good Night, Ladies:* (a) single chord; (b) last two phrases.
(11) *God Give Ye Merry Christmastide:* first and last phrases.
(12) *Rio Grande:* first phrase.

CHAPTER SEVEN

Hymn-Style Accompaniments

HYMNS, MOST PATRIOTIC SONGS AND SOME FOLK SONGS ARE OF SUCH a musical nature that they are not amenable to the types of figuration presented in Chapter 2. The strongly rhythmic character of figured accompaniments is too frivolous for the serious content of the texts; and the harmonic rhythm, frequently requiring a change of chord for almost every melody note, does not lend itself to figuration. Tunes of this type constitute a significant part of our musical heritage, and there are numerous occasions when the accompanist is called on to play them. There are many collections of such songs—arranged in the traditional four parts—available for the accompanist who has had a considerable background in piano technique. For the musician whose background in piano study has been limited, the following three-part arrangements of some of the most familiar songs of the type under discussion will prove useful.

ASSIGNMENT NO. 7

Play the following songs (preferably from memory) accurately and in a tempo and manner suitable for the accompaniment of group singing. Precede each song with an appropriate introduction in three-part chordal style.

1.

Old Hundredth

Louis Bourgeois
Arranged by William Pelz

2. Joseph Mohr

Silent Night

Franz Gruber
Arranged by William Pelz

3. Samuel Francis Smith   *America*   Henry Carey
Arranged by William Pelz

4. Katherine Lee Bates   *America the Beautiful*   Samuel A. Ward
Arranged by William Pelz

ACCOMPANIMENT IMPROVISATION   **43**

5. Francis Scott Key   *The Star-Spangled Banner*   John Stafford Smith
Arranged by William Pelz

ACCOMPANIMENT IMPROVISATION

Home on the Range

American Folk Song
Arranged by William Pelz

ACCOMPANIMENT IMPROVISATION   **45**

CHAPTER EIGHT

Accompaniments with More Sonority and Stronger Rhythmic Movement

THE ACCOMPANIST WILL SOMETIMES ENCOUNTER PROBLEMS FOR which the close-position, tightly-figured keyboard patterns of the preceding chapters are not the best solution. In halls, auditoriums and gymnasiums of vast dimensions, and when large groups of singers are performing, accompaniments with a higher degree of resonance and rhythmic vitality are indicated. One of the most effective ways of providing these elements is as follows:

(a) The left hand plays the chord root in octaves in the lower register of the keyboard, on the first beat of the measure.
(b) The left hand then continues with the full chord, close position, on each of the subsidiary beats of the measure. These afterbeat chords may be in the practical playing positions used before, or in either of the other two close positions possible for each chord. The afterbeat chords should fall within the octave immediately below middle C on the keyboard (occa-

sionally the top note[s] of afterbeat chords may fall somewhat above middle C, but not so high as to cross above the melody being played by the right hand).

(c) The right hand plays the melody in octaves, which may be filled in with one or two notes of the prevailing chord on strong beats, and wherever else it is practical to do so.

The above practice is most useful in $\frac{4}{4}$, $\frac{3}{4}$ and slow $\frac{2}{4}$ meters. In fast $\frac{2}{4}$ and $\frac{6}{8}$ the movement is often too rapid to be practical from the standpoint of the technical demands on the accompanist.

EXAMPLE 25(A). ORIGINAL MELODY IN $\frac{3}{4}$ METER.

EXAMPLE 25(B). OPEN STYLE ACCOMPANIMENT TO EXAMPLE 25(A).

---

(1) For deeper sonority, play the first-beat octaves occasionally an octave lower.

EXAMPLE 26(A). ORIGINAL MELODY IN ⁴⁄₄ METER.

La Golondrina
N. Serradell

EXAMPLE 26(B). OPEN STYLE ACCOMPANIMENT TO EXAMPLE 26(A).

Note that, as in the penultimate measure of Example 26(b) above, when more than one chord to a measure is indicated, the figuring is shortened.

ASSIGNMENT NO. 8

Play the following melodies with accompaniments in the style of Examples 25(b) and 26(b). Precede each example with an introduction in the same style. Opportunities for the use of V_7 of V and V_7 of IV are numerous. Exercises are given in all the commonly used major and minor keys.

1. *A la valse*

Waltz
Victor Herbert

2. *Slowly*

Massa's in de Cold, Cold Ground
Stephen Collins Foster

3. *Molto moderato*

Old Song
Peter Ilyitch Tschaikowsky

4. *Slow waltz*

Will of the Wisp Waltz
Johann Strauss

5. *Moderato*

Cowboy Song
Traditional

6. *Brightly* (Play two chords to each measure)

Country Gardens
Old English Folk Song

Eb: I   IV   V₇   I   etc.

7. *Con moto*

My Bonnie
Traditional

8. *Moderato* (Play two chords to each measure)

Romance
Robert Schumann

IV   I   V₇   I   etc.

9. *Moderato*

Carry Me Back to Old Virginny
James A. Bland

10. *Waltz tempo*

Dolores Waltz
Emil Waldteufel

CHAPTER NINE

Developed Accompaniments

SIMPLICITY IS THE EARMARK OF ALL FOLK MUSIC, AS WELL AS OF many of the famous melodies composed for singing and dancing. The simplicity of the block chord and figured accompaniments studied in the preceding chapters is appropriate, and their modest textures are entirely adequate for the playing of backgrounds to melodies of the folk type. Lyric appeal is so regnant in folk melodies that we are satisfied to hear in the accompaniment merely an unpretentious statement of the harmonic and rhythmic aspects of the music. Then, too, the limited instrumental technique of the folk performer has made simplicity of accompaniment a historic necessity.

For the professional and the accomplished amateur, however, there are many opportunities for achieving a higher degree of musical interest in both the texture and the sonority of the accompaniment. The intelligent use of non-harmonic tones and chord inversions will make possible more melodic bass lines and more varied sonorities. Employment of the secondary triads (II, III, VI), of their respective dominants (V_7 of II, V_7 of III, V_7 of VI), and of occasional altered notes in the principal triads (raised 5th in I and V; lowered 3rd in IV) will add color to the harmony. More elaborate figurations in the left hand and figurations divided between the hands offer almost limitless possibilities for diversity of rhyth-

53

mic character in the accompaniment. The introduction of occasional imitative motives in the lower voices of the accompaniment will serve to integrate the melody with its background. These devices, in tasteful combinations and used with musical discretion, will add to an accompaniment's effectiveness without distorting the essential character of the music.

EXAMPLE 27. MELODY NOTES OCCURRING ON THE BEAT; ACCOMPANIMENT CHORDS ON AFTERBEATS, DIVIDED BETWEEN THE HANDS; USE OF INVERSIONS (I_6 AND V_3^4).

EXAMPLE 28. REPEATED ACCOMPANIMENT CHORDS, DIVIDED BETWEEN THE HANDS, ON AFTERBEATS; USE OF INVERSION (II_6); USE OF SECONDARY DOMINANTS (V_7 of II, V_7 of III, V_7 of IV); CHROMATIC PASSING NOTE.

(1) Chromatic passing note in accompaniment.

EXAMPLE 29. EXTENDED LEFT-HAND ARPEGGIO FIGURATION; MELODY IN BOTH SINGLE NOTES AND OCTAVES; USE OF INVERSIONS (IV$^6_4$ AND V$^4_3$); USE OF SECONDARY TRIADS (III AND VI); USE OF SECONDARY DOMINANT (V$_7$ OF III); USE OF PEDAL TO SUSTAIN EXTENDED LEFT-HAND CHORDS.

Allegretto

Nocturne
J. Leybach

EXAMPLE 30. OPEN LEFT-HAND ARPEGGIO FIGURATION; USE OF INVERSIONS (V_2^4, V_5^6, II_3^4); USE OF SECONDARY DOMINANT (V_7 OF IV); USE OF II_7—A SUBDOMINANT CLASS CHORD SUBSTITUTING FOR IV; USE OF NON-HARMONIC TONES (SUSPENSION, NEIGHBORING [AUXILIARY] TONE); USE OF PEDAL TO SUSTAIN EXTENDED LEFT-HAND CHORDS.

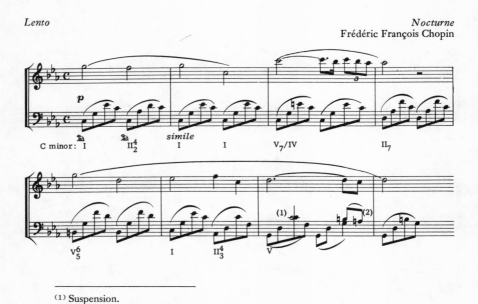

Lento

Nocturne
Frédéric François Chopin

(1) Suspension.
(2) Neighboring (auxiliary) tone.

EXAMPLE 31. DESCENDING ARPEGGIO FIGURATION DIVIDED BETWEEN THE HANDS; USE OF PEDAL TO SUSTAIN ACCOMPANIMENT CHORDS.

NOTE IN THIS EXAMPLE, AND OTHERS GIVEN, THE USUAL AVOIDANCE OF SMALL INTERVALS (3RDS AND 4THS) AT THE BOTTOM OF LEFT-HAND ARPEGGIOS, FOR REASONS OF GOOD SONORITY.

Andantino

Lullaby
Friedrich Burgmüller

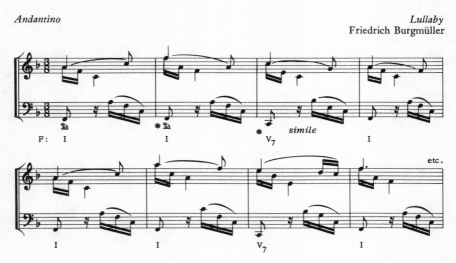

EXAMPLE 32. REPEATED AFTERBEAT ACCOMPANIMENT CHORDS DIVIDED BETWEEN THE HANDS; USE OF SECONDARY TRIAD (II); USE OF INVERSIONS OF SECONDARY DOMINANTS (V_5^6 OF II, V_5^6 OF IV); USE OF INVERSIONS (II_5^6, I_4^6). NOTE HOW THE USE OF INVERSIONS ACHIEVES A SMOOTHLY ASCENDING STEPWISE BASS LINE IN THE ACCOMPANIMENT.

EXAMPLE 33. MOTIVIC IMITATION IN THE ACCOMPANIMENT. NOTE THAT MOTIVE A IS IMITATED AN OCTAVE BELOW IN THE TENOR, AND MOTIVE B IS IMITATED AN OCTAVE AND A FIFTH BELOW IN THE BASS. IMITATION MAY OCCUR AT ANY INTERVAL BELOW THE MELODY, PROVIDED IT FITS THE PREVAILING HARMONY. IT MAY OCCUR IN ANY PART BELOW THE MELODY LINE. IN THE EXAMPLES OF IMITATION GIVEN BELOW, MOTIVE A IS IMMEDIATELY FOLLOWED BY ITS IMITATION; THE IMITATION OF MOTIVE B OVERLAPS THE ORIGINAL STATEMENT OF THE MOTIVE ONE NOTE (*stretto*).

EXAMPLE 34. MOTIVIC IMITATION IN THE ACCOMPANIMENT. NOTE THAT MOTIVE A IS IMITATED AN OCTAVE BELOW; MOTIVE B AN OCTAVE AND A FOURTH BELOW; MOTIVE C AN OCTAVE AND A SECOND BELOW. THE PREVAILING CHORD DETERMINES THE INTERVAL(S) AT WHICH IMITATION IS POSSIBLE.

Old French Song
Peter Ilyitch Tschaikowsky
Arranged by William Pelz

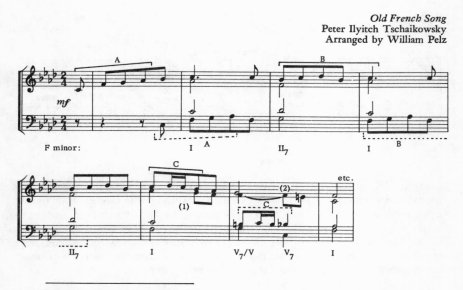

(1) Passing note in accompaniment.
(2) Suspension in accompaniment.

ASSIGNMENT NO. 9

Play the following melodies with accompaniments in the styles indicated. Precede each example with an introduction in the style of the accompaniment used. Suggested harmonies are indicated below each melody. Preceding each exercise is a list of chords used, given in root position on the treble staff, in order of appearance. All commonly used major and minor keys are included.

1. Accompaniment in the style of Example 27:

G: I   IV   V₇/II   II   V₇   V₇/VI   V₇/V   V

Con moto

Minuet
Victor Herbert

G: I   I   IV   V₇/II   II

II   V₇   V₇   V₇/VI   V₇/II

II   V₇/V   V   I   V₇/V   V₇   I

2. Accompaniment in the style of Example 28:

F: I   V₇   VI   V₇/V

Cantabile

Melody from *Martha*
Friedrich von Flotow

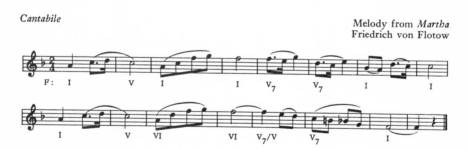

F: I   V   I   I   V₇   V₇   I   I

I   V   VI   VI   V₇/V   V₇   I

3. Accompaniment in the style of Example 29:

C: I   IV V_7 III V_7/III V_7/V

Cantando

Melody from *Mignon*
Ambroise Thomas

C: I   IV V_7 I   I

III V_7/III   III V_7 I   IV V_7

I   I   III V_7/V V_7 I

4. Accompaniment in the style of Example 31:

F minor: I V_7 IV

Moderato

Air
Alessandro Scarlatti

F minor: I V_7 I   IV   I   IV   I V_7

I V_7 I   IV   I   IV I_4^6 V_7 I

5.   Accompaniment in the style of Example 30:

Eb: I   VI   II   V₇   I(lowered 3rd)   V   V₇/V   V   V₇/II

Andante   *Adoration*
                                                    Felix Borowski

Eb: {   I   I₆   VI   II   V₇

  I   I   V₆/V   V₇/V   V   II   V₇   I
      (lowered 3rd)

  II   V₇   I   I₆   V₇/II II   V₇   I

6.   Accompaniment using occasional imitation (see Examples 33 and 34):

F: I   V   V₇

Moderato   *Gavotte*
                                                     G. B. Martini

F: {   {   I   I   I   V   {   {

  I   I   I   V₇   I

7. Accompaniment in the style of Example 29:

C minor: I   IV   V₇/V   V₇   V₇/IV

Moderato   *Waltz*
                                                Hugo Reinhold

8. Accompaniment in the style of Example 27:

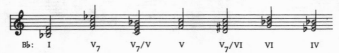

Bb: I   V₇   V₇/V   V   V₇/VI   VI   IV

Andante   Melody from *Rigoletto*
                                        Giuseppe Verdi

9. Accompaniment in the style of Example 30:

C: I   IV   V₇/V   V₇   V₇/VI   V₇/II   V₇/IV   IV (lowered 3rd)

Con amor   *Gypsy Love Song*
                                        Victor Herbert

10. Accompaniment in the style of Example 27:

G minor: I V_7 V_7/VI VI   III IV_7 VI_7(raised root) V_7/V

Cantando

Chanson Triste
Peter Ilyitch Tschaikowsky

G minor: I V_7 I V_7/VI VI   III

IV_7 V_7 I V_7 I VI_7 V_7/V V_7 I
(raised root)

11. Accompaniment in the style of Example 28:

D: I V_7/II II V_7 II_7 V V_7/V

Con espressione

Sweet Dreams
Peter Ilyitch Tschaikowsky

D: I V_7/II V_7 II_2^4 V_6 V_6 V_3^4/V V_7

I V_7/II II V_7 II_2^4 V_5^6 I II_6 V_7 I

12. Accompaniment in the style of Example 31:

A♭: I   IV V_7/V V

Con moto

German Folk Song

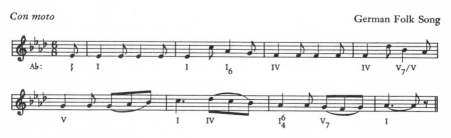

A♭:   I   I I_6 IV   IV V_7/V

V   I   IV I_4^6 V_7 I

ACCOMPANIMENT IMPROVISATION

13. Hymn Style (4 parts):

A: I   V   IV   VI   II   V/VI   V₇/II   V₇/V   V₇   V₇/IV   IV   V/III

Lento

Morning Prayer
Peter Ilyitch Tschaikowsky

A: I   I   V   IV₆   I   V   VI   II₆   V/VI   v⁶₅/II   V₇/V

v⁶₅   I   V⁴₃   I₆   IV   V⁶₅/V   V   I   I   V   IV₆   I   V⁴₂/IV   IV₆   I⁶₄   IV

V/III   V⁴₂/VI   V⁶₅/II   V⁴₂/V   V₆   I   IV₆   IV   V₇   I

14. Accompaniment in the style of Example 27:

G: I   V(raised 5th)   V₇/V   V₇   VI   V   V₇/II   V₇/IV   IV   II

Andante

Berceuse
Moritz Moszkowski

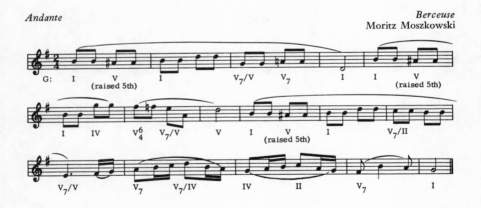

G: I   V (raised 5th)   I   V₇/V   V₇   I   I   V (raised 5th)

I   IV   v⁶₄   V₇/V   V   I   V (raised 5th)   I   V₇/II

V₇/V   V₇   V₇/IV   IV   II   V₇   I

15. Accompaniment in the style of Example 32:

E minor: I   IV   V₇/V   V   V/III   III   V(lowered 3rd)

Moderato

Requiem
Stephen Heller

E minor: I   I   IV   v⁶₅/V   V   I

V   I   V   I   V/III   III   I₆   v⁶₄   V₇/V   V
                                        (lowered 3rd)   (lowered 3rd)

16. Hymn Style (4 parts):

E: I   V₇/IV   IV   V₇/V   II   V₇/II   V   V₇

Andante

Child's Prayer
Theodore Kullak

E: I   V₂⁴/IV   IV₆   IV₆   I₄⁶   V⁶₅/V   II₆   I₆   II

I   v⁶₅/II   v⁶₄   V₇/V   V   ‡   ‡   I   V₂⁴/IV   IV₆   IV₆   I₄⁶

v⁶₅/V   V₂⁴   I₆   II   I   V₇/IV   IV   II   I₄⁶   V₇   I
                            (raised 5th)

17. Accompaniment using occasional imitation (see Examples 33 and 34):

A minor: V₇   I   V₇/V   V

Moderato

Scherzo
Hugo Reinhold

A minor: V₇   I   V₇   I   V₇   I   V₇/V   V

V₇/V   V   V₇/V   V   V₇   I   V₇   I

ACCOMPANIMENT IMPROVISATION   **65**

PART TWO

TRANSPOSITION

CHAPTER TEN

Transposition Up a Half Step to a Key with the Same Letter Name

IN THE COURSE OF HIS DUTIES IN THE CLASSROOM, THE STUDIO, THE church and the rehearsal hall the accompanist is often required to transpose. A vocal soloist may feel that the tessitura of a particular song as originally composed is too low for the most effective use of his voice. A conductor may wish to exploit the increased brilliance resulting from raising the pitch of a choral work. Situations such as these frequently indicate transposition up a half step.

When transposition is made up a half step to a key with the same letter name, the following key changes are possible:

MAJOR KEYS

From C up a half step to C♯
From D♭ up a half step to D
From E♭ up a half step to E
From F up a half step to F♯
From G♭ up a half step to G
From A♭ up a half step to A
From B♭ up a half step to B

From C minor up a half step to C♯ minor
From E♭ minor up a half step to E minor
From F minor up a half step to F♯ minor
From A♭ minor up a half step to A minor
From B♭ minor up a half step to B minor

Transposition up a half step to a key with the same letter name is a simple matter of reading. Three steps are required:

(1) Mental substitution of the new key signature;
(2) Reading the notes as originally written;
(3) Mental substitution of accidentals a half step higher than originally written:

      (a) ♯ becomes 𝄪;
      (b) ♮ becomes ♯;
      (c) ♭ becomes ♮;
      (d) ♭♭ becomes ♭.

(A double sharp in the original will rarely occur in the context of a key to be transposed up a half step to a key with the same letter name.)

EXAMPLE 35(A). EXCERPT IN THE ORIGINAL KEY OF B♭ MAJOR.

Andante Grazioso
Franz Joseph Haydn

EXAMPLE 35(B). TRANSPOSITION UP A HALF STEP TO B MAJOR.

Compare Examples 35 (a) and 35 (b) above, and note:

(1) The change in key signature;
(2) The absence of change in the written notes;
(3) The changes in accidentals:

      (a) F♯ has become F ✗;
      (b) F♮ and B♮ have become respectively F♯ and B♯;
      (c) A♭ has become A♮.

EXAMPLE 36(A). EXCERPT IN THE ORIGINAL KEY OF C MINOR.

EXAMPLE 36(B). TRANSPOSITION UP A HALF STEP TO C♯ MINOR.

Compare Examples 36 (a) and 36 (b) above, and note:

(1) The change in key signature;
(2) The absence of change in the written notes;
(3) The changes in accidentals:

      (a) F♯ has become F ✗;
      (b) B♮ and A♮ have become respectively B♯ and A♯;
      (c) A♭ has become A♮.

TRANSPOSITION

ASSIGNMENT NO. 10

Transpose each of the following musical examples up a half step to a key with the same letter name.

1.   *Sonatina*
Carl Reinecke

2.   *Minuet*
Georg Friedrich Händel

3.   *Minuet*
Johann Vanhall

4.

5.

6. *Andante*

TRANSPOSITION

7. *Allegro*

Sonatina
Friedrich Kuhlau

8. *Andante con moto*

Allemande
Carl Maria von Weber

9. *Tempo di valse*

Christmas
Peter Ilyitch Tschaikowsky

col pedale

TRANSPOSITION

10. *Lento*   *Nocturne*
                                                     John Field

11. Hymn   *Holley*
                                                     George Hews, 1835

CHAPTER ELEVEN

Transposition Down a Half Step to a Key with the Same Letter Name

WE HAVE NOTED IN CHAPTER 10 THAT INDIVIDUAL DIFFERENCES IN vocal range and problems of tessitura sometimes indicate transposition of a solo or choral accompaniment up a half step. Similarly, transposition down a half step is frequently indicated as a solution to one or both of the same problems—range and tessitura.

When transposition is made down a half step to a key with the same letter name, the following key changes are possible:

MAJOR KEYS

From B down a half step to B♭
From A down a half step to A♭
From G down a half step to G♭
From F♯ down a half step to F
From E down a half step to E♭
From D down a half step to D♭
From C♯ down a half step to C
From C down a half step to C♭

MINOR KEYS

From B minor down a half step to B♭ minor
From A minor down a half step to A♭ minor
From F♯ minor down a half step to F minor
From E minor down a half step to E♭ minor
From C♯ minor down a half step to C minor

Transposition down a half step to a key with the same letter name, like such transposition up a half step, is again a simple matter of reading. The first two steps are the same as before:

(1) Mental substitution of the new key signature;
(2) Reading the notes as originally written.

The third step—accidental substitution—is different; now required is the mental substitution of accidentals a half step *lower* than originally written:

> (a) ♯ becomes ♮;
> (b) ♮ becomes ♭;
> (c) ♭ becomes ♭♭;
> (d) 𝄪 becomes ♯.

(A double flat in the original will rarely occur in the context of a key to be transposed down a half step to a key with the same letter name.)

EXAMPLE 37(A). EXCERPT IN THE ORIGINAL KEY OF G MAJOR.

Little Study
Robert Schumann

EXAMPLE 37(B). TRANSPOSITION DOWN A HALF STEP TO G♭ MAJOR.

Compare Examples 37 (a) and 37 (b) above, and note:

(1) The change in key signature;
(2) The absence of change in the written notes;
(3) The changes in accidentals:

  (a) F♯ and C♯ have become respectively F♮ and C♮;
  (b) F♮ and C♮ have become respectively F♭ and C♭;
  (c) E♭ and B♭ have become respectively E♭♭ and B♭♭.

EXAMPLE 38(A). EXCERPT IN THE ORIGINAL KEY OF A MINOR.

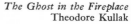

The Ghost in the Fireplace
Theodore Kullak

EXAMPLE 38(B). TRANSPOSITION DOWN A HALF STEP TO A♭ MINOR.

Compare Examples 38 (a) and 38 (b) above, and note:

(1) The change in key signature;
(2) The absence of change in the written notes;
(3) The changes in accidentals:

  (a) G♯ has become G♮;
  (b) B♮ has become B♭;
  (c) B♭ has become B♭♭.

ASSIGNMENT NO. 11

Transpose each of the following musical examples down a half step to a key with the same letter name.

1. *Allegro*

from *Sonata No. 5 in C major*
Franz Joseph Haydn

2. *Moderato*

March of the Dwarfs
Edvard Grieg

3. *Andante*

Chorale
Georg Böhm

4. *Tranquillo*

Variation
Ludwig van Beethoven

TRANSPOSITION

5. *Andante grazioso*

Sonata
Wolfgang Amadeus Mozart

6. *Vivace*

Bourrée
Johann Sebastian Bach

7. *Andante*

Morning Prayer
Peter Ilyitch Tschaikowsky

8. *Allegretto semplice*

Elegie
Edvard Grieg

TRANSPOSITION

9. Hymn

Wentworth
Frederick C. Maker, 1876

10. *Andantino*

Study
Stephen Heller

TRANSPOSITION

CHAPTER TWELVE

Transposition Up a Whole Step

UNLIKE TRANSPOSITION UP OR DOWN A HALF STEP TO A KEY WITH the same letter name, transposition to other intervals is a matter of analysis as well as one of reading. While more complex procedures are involved, these procedures apply to all the intervals of transposition to be studied from this point. The present chapter will limit itself to a discussion of transposition up a whole step—another useful transposition in the accompaniment of solo and ensemble vocal music.

The two essentials for transposition by analysis are:

(1) Complete and accurate analysis of the original music;
(2) Transference to the new key of the elements of musical structure revealed by the analysis.

A large body of two-part and three-part keyboard music is amenable to analysis almost entirely in terms of three structural concepts:

(1) Scale complexes;
(2) Broken chord complexes;
(3) Interval complexes.

EXAMPLE 39(A). ANALYSIS IN TERMS OF SCALE AND BROKEN CHORD COMPLEXES IN THE KEY OF C MAJOR.

Sonatina
Jacob Schmitt

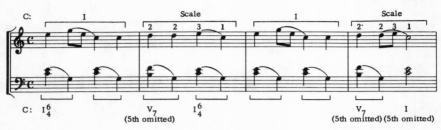

The analysis in this example does not involve the upper staff.

.EXAMPLE 39(B). TRANSPOSITION UP A WHOLE STEP TO D. NOTE THE STRICT TRANS-FERENCE OF ALL COMPLEXES TO THE NEW KEY.

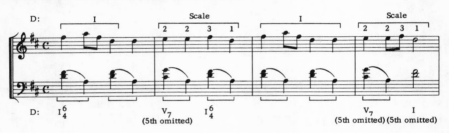

EXAMPLE 40(A). ANALYSIS IN TERMS OF INTERVAL, SCALE AND BROKEN CHORD COM-PLEXES IN THE KEY OF D MINOR.

Minuet
Johann Sebastian Bach

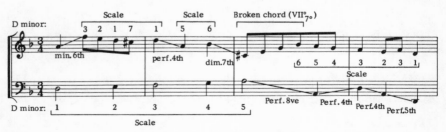

Note that the last two measures of the lower part of Example 40(a) can also be analyzed as scale tones as follows:

84   TRANSPOSITION

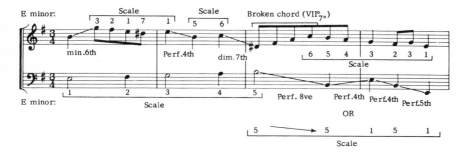

All accidentals in the original are transferred to the new key. Note
below how the raised second and fourth scale degrees in the original
example in F major (41-a) become respectively the raised second and
fourth degrees of the new key of G major (41-b).

EXAMPLE 41(A). ORIGINAL EXAMPLE IN THE KEY OF F MAJOR, WITH ACCIDENTALS.

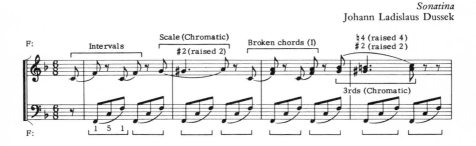

EXAMPLE 41(B). TRANSPOSITION UP A WHOLE STEP TO G MAJOR, SHOWING TRANS-
FERENCE OF ACCIDENTALS TO THE NEW KEY.

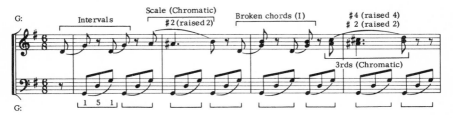

ASSIGNMENT NO. 12

Transpose each of the following musical examples up a whole step. The performance of each transposition should be preceded by a detailed mental (not written) analysis in terms of scale, broken chord and interval complexes.

1. *L'istesso tempo*

Intermezzo
Georg Friedrich Händel

2. *Andante con moto*

Sonatina
Jacob Schmitt

3. *Andante*

Minuet
Johann Sebastian Bach

TRANSPOSITION

4. *Allegro moderato*

5. *Allegro*

6. *Allegro moderato*

7. *Moderato*

TRANSPOSITION

87

8. *Grazioso*

etc.

9. *Leggiero*

Allegro
Domenico Scarlatti

etc.

10. *Vivace*

from *Finale* from *Sonata in E minor*
Franz Joseph Haydn

11. *Allegretto*

from *Sonata in F major*
Wolfgang Amadeus Mozart

TRANSPOSITION

12. *Allegretto*

Variation
Ludwig van Beethoven

13. *Allegretto con moto*

Study
Stephen Heller

TRANSPOSITION

CHAPTER THIRTEEN

Transposition Down a Whole Step

WHEN A SOLOIST ON A B♭ INSTRUMENT PLAYS FROM THE SAME PIANO score as the accompanist, the accompanist must transpose the keyboard part *down* a whole step. The B♭ instruments involved in this transposition are:

> B♭ clarinet
> Bass clarinet
> B♭ trumpet or cornet
> B♭ tenor saxophone

Transposition down a whole step, like the intervals of transposition discussed in preceding chapters, is also frequently indicated for solo or ensemble vocal music.

Four-part music, as well as much three-part music, often requires analysis in terms of chord structure and harmonic progression, in addition to analysis in terms of the interval, scale and broken-chord complexes discussed in Chapter 12. Note in the following example how the melody line, while analyzable exclusively in terms of scale and interval complexes, is also—at the points of rhythmic stress—included in the harmonic analysis.

EXAMPLE 42(A). ANALYSIS IN TERMS OF CHORD STRUCTURE AND HARMONIC PROGRESSION, AS WELL AS SCALE AND INTERVAL COMPLEXES; F MAJOR.

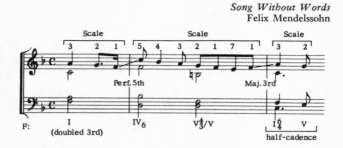

In Example 42(a) above the analysis recognizes:

The unusual doubling in the first chord;
The appoggiatura in the second chord;
Other non-harmonic tones;
The traditional half-cadence formula.

The more detailed the analysis of the original example, the more accurate the transposition which will result.

EXAMPLE 42(B). TRANSPOSITION DOWN A WHOLE STEP TO Eb MAJOR.

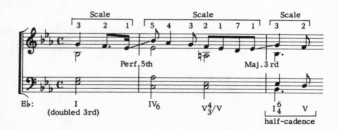

Doubling, spacing, chord position and chord inversion are important elements for giving insight into the harmonic nature of many passages. In Example 43(a) following we find a musical statement of considerable length built entirely on the I chord in the key of Bb major. Note the following:

(1) The melody, beginning on the third of the chord, ascends by skipping up to the fifth, octave, and higher third;
(2) The bass line shows root position, first inversion, root position again and finally the second inversion;

92   TRANSPOSITION

(3) Movement from measure one to measure two is effected by the outside voices (bass and soprano) ascending in skips of thirds, while the inside voices (alto and tenor) hold the same notes;

(4) From this point to the end of the excerpt the bass skips *down* the consecutive notes of the B♭ chord, and the two upper voices (soprano and alto) skip *up* in the same manner;

(5) The tenor holds the same note (the fifth of the key) throughout the entire passage;

(6) All doublings are commonly used ones:

        (a) Root position chords double the root;
        (b) First inversion chord doubles the fifth;
        (c) Second inversion chord doubles the fifth.

EXAMPLE 43(A). EXCERPT SUSCEPTIBLE TO ANALYSIS IN TERMS OF DOUBLING, SPACING, CHORD POSITION AND CHORD INVERSION; B♭ MAJOR.

EXAMPLE 43(B). TRANSPOSITION DOWN A WHOLE STEP TO A♭ MAJOR.

A two-part texture will often imply three-part harmony. Quicker and more accurate reading and transposition are possible when such a passage is read "harmonically" rather than as two lines of single notes.

EXAMPLE 44(A). ORIGINAL EXCERPT WRITTEN AS TWO MELODIC PARTS.

Melody
Robert Schumann

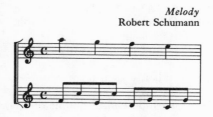

EXAMPLE 44(B). EXAMPLE 44(A) CONVERTED TO THE IMPLIED THREE-PART HARMONY.

C: IV   I₆   V⁴₃   I
                        (chord 3rd
                         omitted)

EXAMPLE 44(C). EXAMPLE 44(B) TRANSPOSED DOWN A WHOLE STEP TO B♭ MAJOR.

B♭:   IV   I₆   V⁴₃   I
                        (chord 3rd
                         omitted)

EXAMPLE 44(D). EXAMPLE 44(C) FIGURED IN THE NEW KEY.

In a similar manner, a two-part texture often implies four-part harmony, as in Example 45 (a) following.

EXAMPLE 45(A). ORIGINAL EXCERPT WRITTEN AS TWO MELODIC PARTS.

Invention
Johann Sebastian Bach

EXAMPLE 45(B). EXAMPLE 45(A) CONVERTED TO THE IMPLIED FOUR-PART HARMONY.

EXAMPLE 45(C). EXAMPLE 45(B) TRANSPOSED DOWN A WHOLE STEP TO G MINOR.

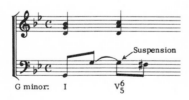

EXAMPLE 45(D). EXAMPLE 45(C) FIGURED IN THE NEW KEY.

TRANSPOSITION

Innumerable combinations of melodic, intervallic and harmonic complexes are to be found in keyboard literature. The following example is a typical combination.

EXAMPLE 46(A). A COMBINATION OF MELODIC AND BROKEN CHORD COMPLEXES.

Music Box
Anatol Liadov

Note in Example 46(a) above, the three components to which the passage is reducible:

(1) A melody composed of both scale and broken chord complexes:

(2) A linear left-hand part convertible to three-part harmony:

(3) Two inside sustained lines:

Combined and transposed down a whole step to G major, these three ingredients result in the following:

EXAMPLE 46(B). TRANSPOSED CONVERSION OF EXAMPLE 46(A).

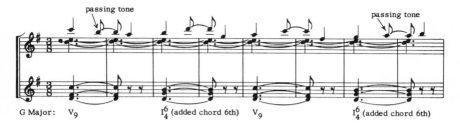

EXAMPLE 46(C). EXAMPLE 46(B) RECONVERTED TO ORIGINAL FIGURATION IN THE NEW KEY.

ASSIGNMENT NO. 13

Transpose each of the following musical examples down a whole step. The performance of each transposition should be preceded by a detailed mental (not written) analysis.

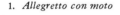

1. *Allegretto con moto*

Study
Stephen Heller

2. *Allegro ma non troppo*

Sonata
Ludwig van Beethoven

3. *Allegro*

Finale
Franz Joseph Haydn

etc.

4. *Moderato*

Serenade
Cécile Chaminade

TRANSPOSITION

5. *Con moto*

Rondo
Johann Ladislaus Dussek

6. *Andante*

Study
Stephen Heller

7. *Moderato*

Minuet
Johann Sebastian Bach

TRANSPOSITION

8. *Poco allegro*

Waltz
Edvard Grieg

etc.

9. *Andante*

Nocturne
John Field

TRANSPOSITION

10. *Moderato*

Siciliano
Johann Sebastian Bach

11. Hymn

Merrial
Joseph Barnby, 1868

TRANSPOSITION

12. Hymn

Evening Prayer
George C. Stebbins, 1878

TRANSPOSITION

CHAPTER FOURTEEN

Transposition to Other Intervals

THE FRENCH HORN AND ENGLISH HORN ARE F INSTRUMENTS. WHEN a soloist on one of these instruments plays from the same piano score as the accompanist, the latter must transpose the piano part down a perfect fifth or up a perfect fourth—whichever places the accompaniment in the most effective register. The alto and baritone saxophones are in E♭, and when a soloist on one of them plays from the same piano score as the accompanist, the accompanying part must be transposed down a major sixth or up a minor third—whichever places the accompaniment in the most effective register.

Vocal soloists and choral directors sometimes find it advisable to raise or lower the key of a particular piece of music as much as a minor or major third. Many piano and organ teachers recommend the transposition of troublesome passages to several other keys, as a means of gaining technical mastery and musical insight.

While the keyboard player must be able to transpose to other keys in order to perform specific duties as a successful accompanist, his greatest advantage from the study of transposition will accrue from increased musicianship—the capacity to grasp instantly the essentials of musical structure to the ends of quick reading, accurate memorization and intelligent interpretation. The great pianist-composer Ferruccio Busoni valued transposition as a discipline so highly that he began each day by transposing a prelude and fugue from J. S. Bach's *Well-Tempered Clavier* to all keys.

The approach to transposition to other intervals than those studied in the preceding chapters is the same as for transposition up or down a whole step. It involves careful and detailed analysis of scale, interval, broken chord and harmonic complexes in the original music, and the transference of these complexes to the new key.

ASSIGNMENT NO. 14

Transpose the following musical examples to the prescribed keys. Precede each transposition with a detailed mental (not written) analysis.

1. *Andante*

Andante
Christoph Willibald von Gluck

Transpose:

(a) Up a minor third;
(b) Up a major third;
(c) Up a perfect fourth.

2. *Moderato*

Transpose:

(a) Down a major 6th;
(b) Down a perfect fifth;
(c) Up a half step.

3. *Animato*

Ecossaise
Ludwig van Beethoven

Transpose:

(a) Up a major third;
(b) Up a perfect fourth;
(c) Down a half step.

TRANSPOSITION 105

Study
Friedrich Burgmüller

Transpose:

(a) Up a minor third;
(b) Down a perfect fifth;
(c) Up a half step.

5. *Moderato*

Andante
Franz Joseph Haydn

Transpose:

(a) Up a major third;
(b) Up a perfect fourth;
(c) Down a half step.

Transpose:

(a) Up a perfect fifth;
(b) Down a major third;
(c) Up a half step.

7. *Allegretto*

Rondo
Jacob Schmitt

Transpose:

(a) Up a major sixth;
(b) Up a minor third;
(c) Up a major third.

8. *Grazioso*

Minuet
Ignaz Joseph Pleyel

Transpose:

(a) Up a half step;
(b) Up a minor third;
(c) Down a major third.

etc.

TRANSPOSITION

9. *Andante*

Transpose:

(a) Down a minor third;
(b) Up a diminished fifth;
(c) Down a perfect fourth.

10. *Tranquillo*

Variation
Ludwig van Beethoven

Transpose:

(a) Down a perfect fifth;
(b) Down a minor third;
(c) Down a half step.

TRANSPOSITION   109

11. Hymn

Beatitudo
John B. Dykes, 1875

Transpose:

(a) Up an augmented fourth;
(b) Up a major third;
(c) Down a half step.

PART THREE

MODULATION

CHAPTER FIFTEEN

Dominant Modulation

MODULATION IS THE PROCESS OF CHANGING KEYS. THERE ARE MANY instances in which the performer at the keyboard is required to modulate —to dissipate the prevailing tonal center and establish a new key-feeling. The singing of a song medley by a soloist or choral group presents the accompanist with problems of modulating between the close of each song and the beginning of the following one. In folk and ballet dance accompaniments, and in the performance of background music to pantomime and other dramatic action, it is necessary to modulate frequently from one musical excerpt to another. The church organist can enhance the unity of the service by connecting certain of its parts with modulations. The studio voice coach finds modulation useful for his accompaniments to the vocalizing of his students. In small dance bands the pianist is expected to supply the modulations involved in moving from tune to tune, or from chorus to chorus.

A new key is effectively established by the progression: dominant—tonic. There are several ways of effecting this progression. The most direct way is to move from the final tonic chord of the old key to the cadence complex: dominant—tonic in the new key.

EXAMPLE 47. DOMINANT MODULATION DOWN A MAJOR SECOND.

Old key (C):I   New key (Bb): V_5^6 I

Development of the ability to play modulations can be accelerated if the modulatory progressions are conceived in visual and tactile terms—in terms of "what happens on the keyboard"—as well as in terms of chord structure and progression. To understand Example 47 in these terms, three concepts are necessary:

(1) The spelling of I in the old key (position, spacing, doubling);
(2) Part movement to the second chord (the intervals of movement in the soprano, alto, tenor, and bass); and
(3) Part movement from the second chord to the third chord.

In Example 47 these three steps would be:

(1) I of the old key is positioned, spaced and doubled as follows:

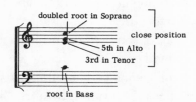

(2) Part by part, movement into the second chord (V_5^6 of the key a major second below) is as follows:

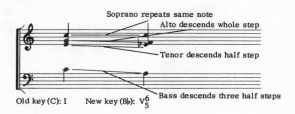

Old key (C): I   New key (Bb): V_5^6

(3) Part by part, movement from the second chord to the third chord is as follows:

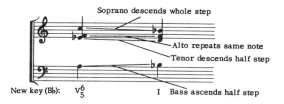

If the three preceding steps are clearly grasped as visual and tactile concepts, as well as in terms of chord structure and progression, the performance of a dominant modulation from any major key to the major key a whole step below is easily done. It is recommended that, in all modulations presented in the following pages, the student consider each one from two points of view:

(1) In terms of theoretical chord structure and progression (chord symbols); and
(2) In terms of "what happens on the keyboard" (the "look" and "feel" of the first chord and the part-by-part movement of each chord into the one following).

Example 47 is given in the spacing of "close position," also known as "keyboard style." This style is suitable for modulations between hymns, or for modulations between songs having the simple accompaniment figurations shown in Part 1 of this text. On the other hand, it is often possible and desirable to put the modulation in the style of the music being played (see Examples 48 and 49). When the new tune exhibits a pianistic figuration, it is advisable to use the figuration of the new piece in the modulation. This makes possible the setting of any different meter and/or tempo the new music might require (see Example 51). In any style, a modulation may be followed by an introduction to the new tune (see Chapter 6).

In practical applications the dominant modulation down a major second, shown in Example 47, leads naturally into melodies beginning either on the tonic note or on the mediant note of the new key.

EXAMPLE 48. DOMINANT MODULATION DOWN A MAJOR SECOND TO A MELODY BEGINNING ON THE TONIC NOTE OF THE NEW KEY (SIMPLE ACCOMPANIMENT STYLE).

EXAMPLE 49. DOMINANT MODULATION DOWN A MAJOR SECOND TO A MELODY BEGINNING ON THE MEDIANT NOTE OF THE NEW KEY (HYMN STYLE).

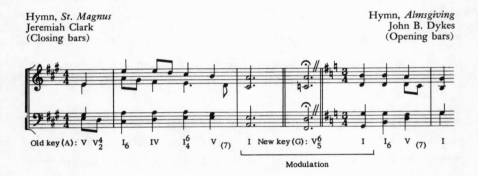

In accompaniments to vocal music, when the new tune begins on the dominant note of the new key, it is advisable for the accompanist to indicate the beginning note at the close of the modulation.

EXAMPLE 50. DOMINANT MODULATION DOWN A MAJOR SECOND TO A MELODY BEGINNING ON THE DOMINANT NOTE OF THE NEW KEY (SIMPLE ACCOMPANIMENT STYLE).

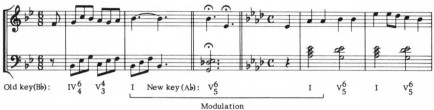

My Bonnie
Scotch song
(Closing bars)

O, No John
English folk song
(Opening bars)

EXAMPLE 51. DOMINANT MODULATION DOWN A MAJOR SECOND (PIANISTIC FIGURATIONS IN BOTH PIECES, WITH THE MODULATION ASSUMING THE FIGURATION, TEMPO AND METER OF THE NEW PIECE).

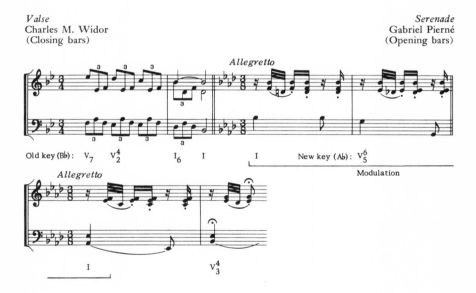

Valse
Charles M. Widor
(Closing bars)

Serenade
Gabriel Pierné
(Opening bars)

Dominant modulation from a major key to the major key lying a *major third below* is achieved by continuing the progression given in Example 47.

EXAMPLE 52. DOMINANT MODULATION DOWN A MAJOR THIRD.

EXAMPLE 53. PRACTICAL APPLICATION OF EXAMPLE 52 (HYMN STYLE).

Hymn, *Mozart*
Wolfgang Amadeus Mozart
(Closing bars)

Hymn, *Hollingside*
John B. Dykes
(Opening bar)

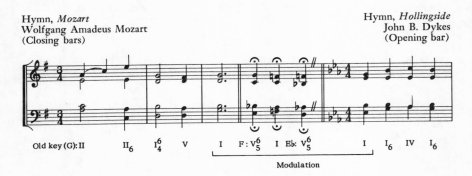

The following example shows a dominant modulation from one major key to another major key lying a *minor third below*. Note that, while the new key has been satisfactorily established by the time the third chord has sounded, the fact that the seventh of the new dominant chord occurs in the soprano intimates that the forthcoming melody will begin on the mediant note of the new key. To adapt the modulation to melodies beginning on *either* the mediant note or the tonic note of the new key, the cadence complex has been restated with the V_5^6 chord positioned so that its fifth is in the soprano. Should the new melody begin on the dominant note of the new key, this note should be sounded at the close of the modulation, as shown in Example 50 (vocal accompaniments).

EXAMPLE 54. DOMINANT MODULATION DOWN A MINOR THIRD.

EXAMPLE 55. PRACTICAL APPLICATION OF EXAMPLE 54 (FIGURED STYLE).

German Dance
Franz Schubert
(Closing bars)

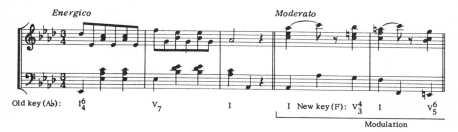

German Dance
Ludwig Van Beethoven
(Opening bars)

ASSIGNMENT NO. 15

A. (1) Continue the following modulating sequence (developed from Example 47) until a return is made to the original key (C):

MODULATION   119

(2) Continue the following modulating sequence (developed from Example 47) until a return is made to the original key (B):

B: I   A: V⁶₅   I   G: V⁶₅   I   F: V⁶₅   etc.

(3) Continue the following modulating sequence (developed from Example 54) until a return is made to the original key (C):

C: I   A: V⁴₃   I   V⁶₅   I   F♯: V⁴₃   I   V⁶₅   I   E♭: V⁴₃   etc.

(4) Play the sequence pattern given in number 3 above, beginning in D♭, and continuing until a return is made to D♭.

(5) Play the sequence pattern given in number 3 above, beginning in D, and continuing until a return is made to D.

B.   Each of the following exercises consists of: (a) the *closing* bars of a song or piece in a major key, and (b) the *opening* bars of another song or piece in the major key a whole step (major second) below. In each instance the two excerpts are to be connected by means of the dominant modulation given in Example 47. Remember that, in vocal accompaniments, when the second melody begins on the dominant note of the new key, this note must be played at the close of the modulation. Remember also that, in both vocal and instrumental music, figurations and changes of tempo and/or meter in the forthcoming music should be anticipated in the modulation. Play modulations between hymns in hymn style (open harmony).

1. *Reuben, Reuben*
   Folk Song
   (Closing bars)

Li'l Liza Jane
Folk Song
(Opening bars)

2. *Hark, the Herald Angels Sing*   *Deck the Hall*
   Felix Mendelssohn   Welsh carol
   (Closing bars)   (Opening bars)

3. *Crusader's Hymn*
   Silesian Folk Song
   (Closing bars)

(Use tempo and figuration of second tune in the modulation)

Cantique de Noel
Adolphe Adam
(Opening bars)

MODULATION   **121**

4. *Rondo*
Muzio Clementi
(End of excerpt)

Valse
Peter Ilyitch Tschaikowsky
(Beginning of excerpt)

(Use tempo, meter and figuration of second tune in the modulation)

C. Each of the following exercises consists of: (a) the closing bars of a song or piece in a major key, and (b) the opening bars of another song or piece in the major key lying a major third below. In each instance the two excerpts are to be connected by means of the dominant modulation given in Example 52. Keep in mind the special treatments required for new melodies beginning on the fifth of the new key, and for changes in tempo, meter and figuration.

1. *Tavern in the Town*
American Folk Song
(Closing bars)

Who Will Shoe Your Pretty Little Foot?
American Folk Song
(Opening bars)

2. Hymn, *St. Anne*
William Croft (?)
(Closing bars)

Hymn, *Need*
Robert Lowry
(Opening bars)

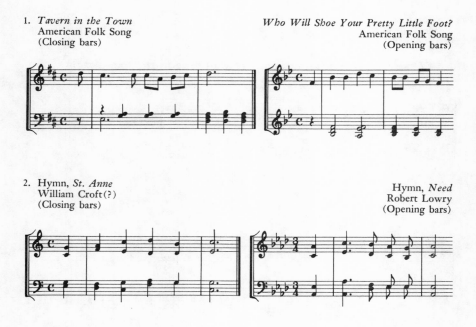

MODULATION

3. *Ring, Ring de Banjo*
   Stephen Foster
   (Closing bars)

Funiculi, Funicula
Luigi Denza
(Opening bars)

4. *Song*
   Felix Mendelssohn
   (Closing bars)

Nazareth
Charles Gounod
(Opening bars)

MODULATION

D. Each of the following exercises consists of: (a) the closing bars of a song or piece in a major key, and (b) the opening bars of a different song or piece in the major key a minor third below. In each instance the two excerpts are to be connected by means of the dominant modulation given in Example 54. Keep in mind the special treatments required for new melodies beginning on the fifth tone of the new key, and for changes in tempo, meter and figuration.

1. *Passing By*
   Edward Purcell
   (Closing bars)

Moderato

Little Folksong
Robert Schumann
(Opening bars)

Con moto

2. Hymn, *Germany*
   William Gardiner
   (Closing bars)

Hymn, *Coronation*
Oliver Holden
(Opening bars)

3. *Ave Maria*
   Pietro Mascagni
   (Closing bars)

Ave Maria
Bach-Gounod
(Opening bars)

4. *German Dance*
   Ludwig van Beethoven
   (End of excerpt)

Dance Caprice
Edvard Grieg
(Opening bars)

CHAPTER SIXTEEN

Pivot Modulation

Wʜᴇɴ ᴛᴡᴏ ᴋᴇʏs ʜᴀᴠᴇ sᴇᴠᴇʀᴀʟ ɴᴏᴛᴇs ɪɴ ᴄᴏᴍᴍᴏɴ (ᴀɴᴅ, ᴄᴏɴsᴇ-
quently, chords in common) it is possible to modulate from one key to
the other by means of a common (pivot) chord. The pivot chord serves
both as a means of departure from the old key and a means of entrance
into the new key. The new tonality is confirmed either by the cadence
complex: dominant—tonic, or by the more definitive complex: I_4^6-V_7-I.

EXAMPLE 56. ᴘɪᴠᴏᴛ ᴍᴏᴅᴜʟᴀᴛɪᴏɴ ᴅᴏᴡɴ ᴀ ᴘᴇʀғᴇᴄᴛ ғᴏᴜʀᴛʜ.

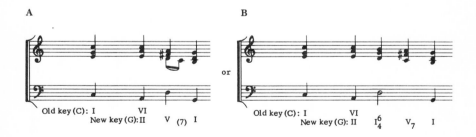

A
B

or

Old key (C): I   VI
New key (G): II   V (7)   I

Old key (C): I   VI
New key (G): II I_4^6 V_7 I

In each of the examples above, the second chord is a pivot chord,
functioning both as VI in the old key and as II in the new key. In practical applications this progression (and all succeeding modulatory progressions to be presented) can be suitably adapted to either hymn style

(open harmony) or to pianistic figured style. However, all succeeding modulations between tunes in simple accompaniment style (see Chapters 1 through 6) should be played in the close position style exemplified by Example 56 above. Succeeding modulations will use chords other than the basic ones characteristic of folk and dancing music; these chords do not adapt easily—from the standpoint of voice leading—to simple accompaniment style.

Like the modulations presented in Chapter 15, succeeding examples will use a position of the new dominant chord that permits movement into a new melody beginning on either the tonic note or the mediant note of the new key. In all future exercises, when a new melody begins on the dominant note of the new key, this note must be sounded at the close of the modulation (in vocal accompaniments).

EXAMPLE 57(A). PIVOT MODULATION DOWN A PERFECT FOURTH (SIMPLE ACCOMPANIMENT STYLE).

Once I Loved a Maiden
English Folk Song
(Closing bars)

O How Lovely is the Maiden
Robert Schumann
(Opening bars)

EXAMPLE 57(B). PIVOT MODULATION DOWN A PERFECT FOURTH (HYMN STYLE).

Hymn, *Pro Patria*
Horatio W. Parker
(Closing bars)

Hymn, *St. Crispin*
George J. Elvey
(Opening bars)

EXAMPLE 57(C). PIVOT MODULATION DOWN A PERFECT FOURTH (FIGURED STYLE).

O, Press Your Cheek
Adolf Jensen
(Closing bars)

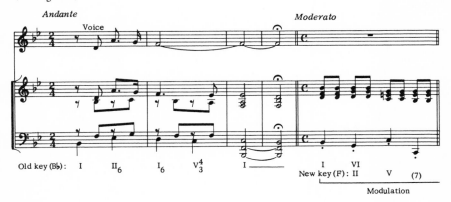

Who Is Sylvia?
Franz Schubert
(Opening bars)

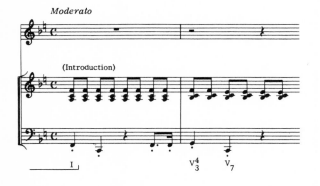

EXAMPLE 58. PIVOT MODULATION DOWN A PERFECT FIFTH.

Old key (C): I   VI
New key (F): III   IV   (I⁶₄)   V (7)   I

The pivot chord in Example 58 above is VI in the old key and III in the new key. Note the cadence complex: IV(I⁶₄)-V₇-I.

EXAMPLE 59. PIVOT MODULATION DOWN A PERFECT FIFTH (HYMN STYLE).

Hymn, *St. Theodulph*
Melchior Teschner
(Closing bars)

Hymn, *Hamburg*
Lowell Mason
(Opening bars)

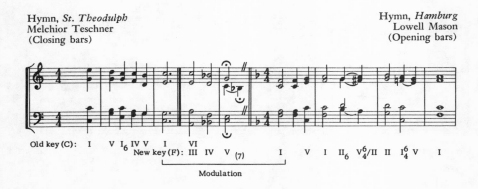

Old key (C): I   V I₆ IV V   I   VI
New key (F):   III IV V (7)   I   V   I   II₆ V⁶₄/II II I⁶₄ V   I

                         ⌊_____⌋
                            Modulation

EXAMPLE 60. PIVOT MODULATION DOWN A MINOR SIXTH.

Old key (C): I   VI
New key (E): IV   (I⁶₄)   V   (7)   I

_____

(1) The C♮ in this chord is a "borrowed tone" from E minor.

The pivot chord in Example 60 above is VI in the old key and IV in the new key.

EXAMPLE 61. PIVOT MODULATION DOWN A MINOR SIXTH (FIGURED STYLE).

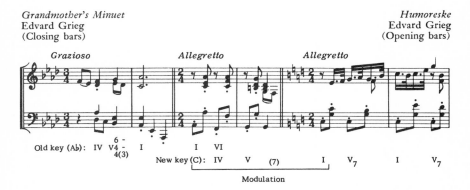

ASSIGNMENT NO. 16

A. Continue the following modulating sequence (developed from Example 56[b]) until a return is made to the original key (C). It will be occasionally necessary to move up to a higher position on the keyboard in order to avoid the undesirably thick sonorities of the extreme low register.

B. Continue the following modulatory sequence (developed from Example 58) until a return is made to the original key (C). Move to a higher register on the keyboard whenever necessary.

MODULATION   131

C. Continue the following modulatory sequence (developed from Example 60) until a return is made to the original key (C).

C: I   VI
        E: IV   V
                (7) I   VI
                  G♯: IV   V
                            (7) [I = A♭: I]   VI
                                        C: IV   V

D. Play the sequence given in Exercise C above, beginning and ending in D♭.

E. Play the same sequence, beginning and ending in D.

F. Play the same sequence, beginning and ending in E♭.

G. Each of the following exercises consists of: (a) the closing bars of a song, hymn or piece in a major key, and (b) the opening bars of another song, hymn or piece in one of the following major keys:

    (a) a perfect fourth lower;
    (b) a perfect fifth lower;
    (c) a minor sixth lower.

Each pair of musical excerpts is to be connected by means of the appropriate modulation. Use the close position style of Example 56 for modulations joining excerpts given in simple accompaniment style; use open harmony for modulations connecting hymn passages; when the second excerpt is figured use the figuration in the modulation, which also must set the new tempo and meter. In vocal accompaniments, when the new tune begins on the dominant note of the new key, this note must be sounded for the singer(s) at the close of the modulation.

1. *Long, Long Ago*
Thomas H. Bayly
(Closing bars)

Kathleen Aroon
Franz Abt
(Opening bars)

2. Hymn, *Pentecost*
William Boyd
(Closing bars)

Hymn, *St. Asaph*
William S. Bambridge
(Opening bars)

3. *You Are So Like a Flower*
Robert Schumann
(Closing bars)

The Lotus Flower
Robert Schumann
(Opening bars)

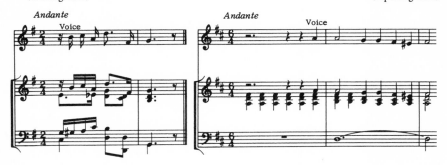

4. *Love Somebody*
American Folk Song
(Closing bars)

Love's Old Sweet Song
J. L. Molloy
(Opening bars)

5. Hymn, *Jubilate*
Horatio Parker
(Closing bars)

Hymn, *St. Agnes*
John B. Dykes
(Opening bars)

6. *Under the Leaves*
Joseph Francois Thomé
(Closing bars)

Dreams
Georges Bizet
(Opening bars)

MODULATION

7. *My Love Is Gone to Sea*
Francis Hopkinson
(Closing bars)

Then You'll Remember Me
Michael William Balfe
(Opening bars)

8. Hymn, *Meditation*
John H. Gower
(Closing bars)

Hymn, *Schumann*
Mason and Webb's *Cantica Laudis*

9. *My Maiden's Lips*
Johannes Brahms
(Closing bars)

Lovely Maiden
Franz Joseph Haydn
(Opening bars)

10. Hymn, *Webb*
George J. Webb
(Closing bars)

Hymn, *Trentham*
Robert Jackson
(Opening bars)

MODULATION

CHAPTER SEVENTEEN

Chromatic Modulation

WHEN ONE OR MORE NOTES OF A CHORD IN THE OLD KEY ARE CHRO-matically changed to produce a chord in the new key, chromatic modulation results. Any chord of the old key may be subjected to such chromatic alteration; however, since we are concerned here only with modulations to new keys *from the closing chord of the old key*, the old-key chord to be chromatically altered will always be the final tonic chord. Also, since brevity is desirable in the practical modulations with which we are concerned, chromatic alterations that convert the old-key I immediately into a dominant chord in the new key—or that result in a chord leading directly to the new cadence complex—are preferable. In a chromatic modulation:

(1) One or more notes of the old-key I are chromatically altered;
(2) One or more notes of the old-key I may be retained;
(3) A new note (a member of the new chord) may be added.

EXAMPLE 62. CHROMATIC MODULATION UP A MINOR THIRD.

Old key (C): I New key (E♭): VII₇/V I⁶₄ V₇ I

135

In Example 62 the final I chord of the old key is converted into VII₇/V of the new key as follows:

(1) E in the alto is chromatically altered to E♭;
(2) G in the soprano and C in the tenor are retained;
(3) A new note from the new chord (A) is added in the bass.

Note that this modulatory progression begins with a position of the old-key I different from that used previously. (In Example 62, the fifth of the old-key I is in the soprano, rather than the root).

EXAMPLE 63. PRACTICAL APPLICATION OF EXAMPLE 62 (FIGURED STYLE).

EXAMPLE 64. CHROMATIC MODULATION UP A MAJOR SECOND.

In all preceding examples of modulation the new-key dominant chord has been V_7. In Example 64 above, the new-key dominant chord is a diminished seventh chord. Note also in Example 64:

136   MODULATION

(1) C in the alto is chromatically altered to C♯;
(2) E in the soprano and G in the tenor are retained;
(3) A new note (B♭) from the new chord is added in the bass.

The old-key I chord has the third in the soprano.

EXAMPLE 65. PRACTICAL APPLICATION OF EXAMPLE 64 (HYMN STYLE).

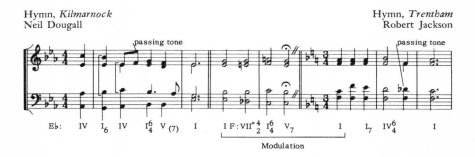

EXAMPLE 66. CHROMATIC MODULATION DOWN A DIMINISHED FIFTH.

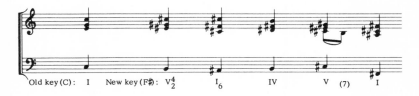

In Example 66 above:

(1) C, G and E in the soprano, alto and tenor are altered respectively to C♯, G♯ and E♯;
(2) No notes are retained;
(3) A new note (B) from the new chord is added in the bass.

Note also the two-cadence complexes in the new key: V_2^4-I_6, and IV-V_7-I.

Come Where My Love Lies Dreaming
Stephen Foster

Farewell to Thee
Queen Liliuokalani

(1) E♯, B♯ and G✕ are notated in the new key (B♭ Major) as F, C and A respectively.

It is interesting to observe that when chromatic modulation is effected by chromatic alteration of the old-key I chord directly into a dominant chord of the new key, such modulation is—by definition—also dominant modulation (see Chapter 15). This is not the case, of course, when:

(1) Some other chord than the old-key I is altered;
(2) The alteration results in a non-dominant chord of the new key (see Example 62).

ASSIGNMENT NO. 17

A. Play the modulation given in Example 62, beginning on the I chord in D♭ (modulation to E). Play the same modulation, beginning on the respective I chords of the following keys: A, E♭, C, F, D, B♭, E, G♭, and A♭ (Note the position of the old-key I chord).

B. Play the modulation given in Example 64, beginning on the I chord in each of the twelve major keys (Note the position of the old-key I chord).

C. Play the modulation given in Example 66, beginning on the I chord in each of the twelve major keys (Note the position of the old-key I chord).

D. Each of the following exercises consists of: (a) the closing bars of a song, hymn or piece in a major key, and the opening bars of another song, hymn or piece in one of the following major keys:

    (a) A minor third higher;
    (b) A major second higher;
    (c) A diminished fifth lower (augmented fourth higher).

Each pair of musical excerpts is to be connected by means of the appropriate modulation. Use close position style for modulations joining excerpts given in simple accompaniment style; use open harmony for modulations between hymns; when the second excerpt is figured, use the figuration (or an adaptation of it) in the modulation, which also must set the new tempo and meter. In vocal accompaniments, when the new tune begins on the dominant note of the new key, this note must be sounded for the singer(s) at the close of the modulation.

1. Melody from *Martha*
   Friedrich von Flotow

Melody from *Martha*
Friedrich von Flotow

2. Hymn, *Wesley*
   Lowell Mason

Hymn, *Crossing the Bar*
Joseph Barnby

3. *Caro Mio Ben*
Giuseppe Giordani

Ich Liebe Dich
Ludwig van Beethoven

4. *Sailor's Hornpipe*
Sea Chantey

Blow the Man Down
Sea Chantey

5. Hymn, *Hermas*
Frances R. Havergal

Hymn, *Regent Square*
Henry Smart

6. *Mazurka*
Frédéric François Chopin

Elegie
Edvard Grieg
(Excerpt)

MODULATION

7. *The First Noël*
Traditional Carol

Good King Wenceslaus
Traditional Carol

8. Hymn, *Swabia*
Johann Spiess

Hymn, *Flemming*
Friedrich Flemming

9. *Waltz*
Hugo Reinhold

Grazioso

Trio
Ludwig van Beethoven

Con moto

10. Hymn, *Martyrdom*
Hugo Wilson

Hymn, *All Saints New*
Henry Cutler

MODULATION

CHAPTER EIGHTEEN

Enharmonic
Modulation

THE GERMAN SIXTH ($\frac{6+}{5}$) IS FREQUENTLY AN ALTERED IV₇ CHORD IN
the minor key. (The minor IV₇ with a raised root):

C: German 6th.

It is most often used in the first inversion, and although its normal progression in the key is either to I$^6_4$ (in minor) or to V (in minor), it can
be used as a means of departure from a *major* key, since it has the sound
of a dominant seventh chord in the key *one half step higher*.

EXAMPLE 68(A). GERMAN SIXTH PROGRESSING TO I_4^6 OR V IN THE KEY (NON-MODU-LATING).

C minor: I   IV$\frac{6+}{3}$5   (I_4^6)   V

EXAMPLE 68(B). GERMAN SIXTH USED ENHARMONICALLY (AS V_7 OF THE KEY A HALF STEP HIGHER) TO MODULATE UP A MINOR SECOND.

Old key (C):   I   IV$\frac{6+}{3}$5 = New key (D♭): V_7 I

EXAMPLE 69. PRACTICAL APPLICATION OF EXAMPLE 68(B) (HYMN STYLE).

Hymn, *St. Peter*
Alexander Reinagle

Hymn, *St. Crispin*
George J. Elvey

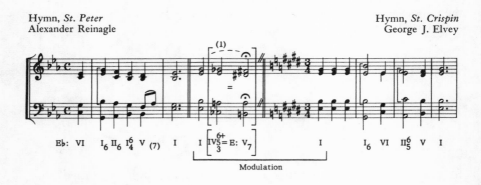

E♭: VI   I$_6$ II$_6$ I$_4^6$ V (7)   I   I [IV$\frac{6+}{3}$5 = E: V_7]   I   I$_6$ VI II$_5^6$ V I

Modulation

---

(1) This chord, although written twice to show enharmonic notation, is to be played only once.

We have seen in Chapter 7 (paragraph following Example 67) that certain modulations can be classified as either dominant or chromatic. The modulation given in Example 68(b) can be classified in three ways:

(a) As a dominant modulation (a progression directly from old-key I to new-key V₇):

$$\text{C: I} \quad \text{D}\flat\text{: V}_7 \qquad \text{I}$$

(b) As a chromatic modulation, exhibiting all three characteristics of this type of modulation:

   (1) The soprano and tenor of old-key I are chromatically altered from E to E♭, and from G to G♭, respectively;

   (2) The alto is retained;

   (3) The bass introduces a new note from the new chord (A♭).

(c) As an enharmonic modulation (see Example 68[b]). In this case the modulating chord functions as a pivot chord which is notated differently in each of the two keys involved.

Example 68(b) has shown that when a chord is *entered as a German Sixth in the old key* and *resolves as a dominant seventh chord of the new key*, modulation to a key *one half step higher* is effected. Conversely, when a chord is *entered as a dominant seventh chord of the old key* and *resolves as a German Sixth in the new key*, a modulation to a key *one half step lower* takes place.

EXAMPLE 70. DOMINANT SEVENTH CHORD USED ENHARMONICALLY (AS $\begin{smallmatrix}6+\\5\\3\end{smallmatrix}$ OF THE KEY A HALF STEP LOWER) TO MODULATE DOWN A MINOR SECOND.

Old key (C): I   [V₇ = New key (B): IV$\begin{smallmatrix}6+\\5\\3\end{smallmatrix}$]   I$^6_4$ V₇   I

EXAMPLE 71. PRACTICAL APPLICATION OF EXAMPLE 70 (SIMPLE ACCOMPANIMENT STYLE).

Old Paint
Cowboy song

Modulation

A Dream Life
Cowboy song

ASSIGNMENT NO. 18

A. Play the modulation given in Example 68(b), beginning on the I chord in each of the twelve major keys. Note the position of the old-key I chord.

B. Play the modulation given in Example 70, beginning on the I chord in each of the twelve major keys. Note the position of the old-key I chord.

C. Each of the following exercises consists of: (a) the closing bars of a song, hymn or piece in a major key, and the opening bars of another song, hymn or piece in one of the following major keys:

    (1) A minor second (half step) higher;
    (2) A minor second (half step) lower.

Each pair of musical excerpts is to be connected by means of the appropriate modulation, performed in an appropriate style.

1. *This Endris Night*
Traditional English melody

Angels We Have Heard on High
Traditional French melody

2. Hymn, *Adeste Fidelis*
J. F. Wade

Hymn, *Mirfield*
Arthur Cottman

3. *Rondo* (excerpt)
Muzio Clementi

Prelude (excerpt)
Johann Kuhnau

4. Hymn, *Azmon*
Carl G. Gläser

Hymn, *North Coates*
Timothy Matthews

5. *Cowboy's Lament*
American Folk Song

Sourwood Mountain
American Folk Song

MODULATION

6. Hymn, *Cowper*
Lowell Mason

Hymn, *Ajalon*
Richard Redhead

7. *Rondo* (excerpt)
Ludwig van Beethoven

Moment Musical No. 3 (excerpt)
Franz Schubert

8. Hymn, *Martyn*
Simeon Marsh

Hymn, *Diademata*
George J. Elvey

MODULATION

CHAPTER NINETEEN

Modulations Involving Minor Keys

COLLECTIVELY THE MODULATIONS PRESENTED IN THE PRECEDING chapters provide the means for moving from any particular major key to any of the remaining major keys. They included examples from four general types of modulation: dominant, pivot, chromatic and enharmonic. It was noted that—depending on definition and notation—certain modulations can be classified as belonging to two, or even three, different types.

In addition to modulating from one major key to another major key, the pianist or organist must frequently modulate in one of the following ways:

(1) From a major key to a minor key;
(2) From a minor key to a major key;
(3) From a minor key to another minor key.

Many of the preceding major-to-major schemes can be adapted to all three modal variants listed above. Since the first chord of all the schemes given in Chapters 15 to 18 is the final tonic chord of the old key, a lowering of the chord third by a half step in the old-key I is sufficient for indicating that the old key is in the minor mode.

To convert the *new* key into the minor mode, all tonic chords (I, I₆, I₆₄) and the subdominant chord (IV) should be made minor by lowering their respective thirds one half step.

The dominant chord in the new key is not changed, since the dominant chords used in the models (V₇, VII°₇) are identical in major keys and minor keys. The examples below demonstrate the modal variants of the modulation down a whole step.

EXAMPLE 72(A). DOMINANT MODULATION FROM A MAJOR KEY TO A MAJOR KEY A WHOLE STEP BELOW (AS ORIGINALLY GIVEN IN EXAMPLE 47, CHAPTER 15).

EXAMPLE 72(B). DOMINANT MODULATION FROM A MAJOR KEY TO A MINOR KEY A WHOLE STEP BELOW.

(1) Note the lowered third in the new-key I.

EXAMPLE 72(C). DOMINANT MODULATION FROM A MINOR KEY TO A MAJOR KEY A WHOLE STEP BELOW.

(1) Note the lowered third in the old-key I.

EXAMPLE 72(D). DOMINANT MODULATION FROM A MINOR KEY TO A MINOR KEY A WHOLE STEP BELOW.

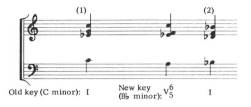

Old key (C minor): I New key (Bb minor): V⁶₅ I

---

(1) Note the lowered third in old-key I.
(2) Note the lowered third in new-key I.

Examples 72(a), (b), (c), and (d) illustrate the principle that, in all modulations, the tonic chord (and the subdominant, if used) defines the mode (major or minor quality) of a key; and that the dominant chord remains the same in either mode. Although only representative examples of dominant modulations have been given in the text, it is possible to modulate from any key (major or minor) to any other key (major or minor) by the dominant process:

Old-key I—New-key dominant—New-key I

The new-key dominant may be V₇, V⁶₅, V⁴₃, V⁴₂; it may be the root position of VII⁷° or any of its inversions; it may be root position or any inversion of the leading-tone seventh chord in major (VII⁷—the "half diminished" seventh chord); it may be V₉ of the new key; V of the new key is an acceptable modulating chord, though not so strong as the other dominant chords listed above.

It is important that the inversion selected for the new-key dominant chord makes possible a smooth progression from old-key I to new-key dominant (keep common tones usually, move parts by step and/or small skip). If this principle is observed, even modulations to remote keys will sound smooth and convincing.

EXAMPLE 73. DOMINANT MODULATION FROM A MAJOR KEY DOWN A MAJOR THIRD TO A MINOR KEY (REMOTELY RELATED).

Old key (C Major): I   New key   V$_3^4$ I   (V$_5^6$ I)
                    (A♭ minor):

---

(1) Note the smooth voice-leading from old-key I to new-key V$_3^4$.

Pivot chord modulations are not as adaptable to changes of mode as are dominant modulations. When the mode of either the old key or of the new key is changed, a change of key-signature takes place that often obliterates the common quality of the pivot chord. Frequently, however, the change of mode does not rule out the acceptability of the modulation. For instance, in Example 58 (Chapter 16) the following illustration of pivot modulation was given:

EXAMPLE 74(A). PIVOT CHORD MODULATION FROM A MAJOR KEY DOWN A PERFECT FIFTH TO A MAJOR KEY (ORIGINALLY EXAMPLE 58, CHAPTER 16).

Old key (C Major): I   VI
                   New key (F Major): III   IV   (I$_4^6$)   V   (7)   I

Changing the mode of the new key from major to minor results in the following:

EXAMPLE 74(B). PIVOT CHORD MODULATION FROM A MAJOR KEY DOWN A PERFECT
FIFTH TO A MINOR KEY.

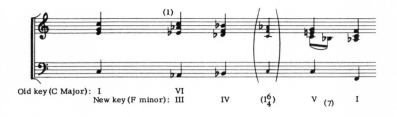

(1) A borrowed chord from C minor.

What makes the foregoing modulation acceptable and convincing
is the fact that *the altered notation of the pivot chord in the new key does
not prevent its being considered as a borrowed chord from the opposite
mode* (C minor) *of the old key.* Example 75 provides another illustration
of this principle:

EXAMPLE 75. MODULATION FROM A MAJOR KEY TO A MINOR KEY A PERFECT FOURTH
BELOW (A MODAL VARIANT OF EXAMPLE 56[B], CHAPTER 16).

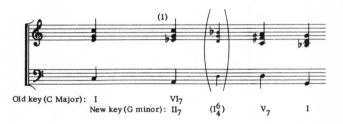

(1) E♭ is a borrowed tone from C minor.

The *Neapolitan Sixth* is a major chord built on the lowered second
degree of the scale:

Its progression within the key is usually from its first inversion to I$^6_4$ or V$_7$ in minor; in these progressions the usual doubling in N$_6$ is the chord third:

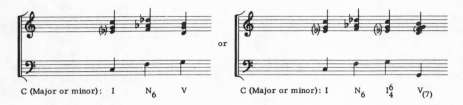

or

C (Major or minor):   I   N$_6$ V   C (Major or minor):   I   N$_6$ I$^6_4$ V$_{(7)}$

In modulating passages, the *root* of N$_6$ is frequently doubled.

The Neapolitan Sixth can be used as a common chord in modulations, either as N$_6$ in the old key, or as N$_6$ in the new key.

EXAMPLE 76. MODULATION FROM A MINOR KEY TO A MAJOR KEY A MAJOR THIRD LOWER, USING N$_6$ OF THE OLD KEY AS A PIVOT CHORD.

Old key (C minor): I   N$_6$
New key (A♭ Major):   IV$_6$ (I$^6_4$)   V$_7$ I

EXAMPLE 77. MODULATION FROM A MAJOR KEY TO A MINOR KEY A MAJOR THIRD HIGHER, USING N$_6$ OF THE NEW KEY AS A PIVOT CHORD.

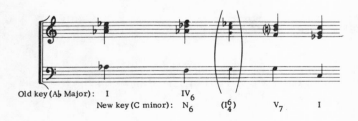

Old key (A♭ Major):   I   IV$_6$
New key (C minor):   N$_6$ (I$^6_4$)   V$_7$ I

Another useful modulation using N$_6$ as a pivot chord is:

Old key (minor) I-$\left(\dfrac{\text{N}_6}{\text{V}_6}\right)$-I-(V$^6_5$-I)$\left.\right\}$ Modulation up a
New key (Major or minor) diminished fifth

The diminished seventh chord, in the key, resolves normally to I, and is used with equal frequency in major and minor:

C (Major or minor): I   VII$^o_7$ I

Any tone (3rd, 5th, 7th) of the old-key VII$^o_7$ may be considered as a leading tone, and the chord resolved to a new tonic (major or minor) whose root is a half-step above the note of the original VII$^o_7$ selected as a leading tone.

EXAMPLE 78(A). MODULATION IN WHICH THE THIRD OF THE OLD-KEY VII$^o_7$ BECOMES THE ROOT OF THE NEW-KEY VII$^o_7$.

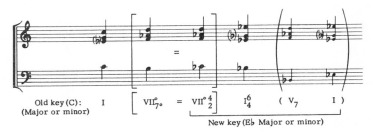

Old key (C):   I   [VII$^o_7$ = VII$^o\,^4_2$ I$^6_4$ (V$_7$ I)]
(Major or minor)

New key (E♭ Major or minor)

EXAMPLE 78(B). MODULATION IN WHICH THE FIFTH OF THE OLD-KEY VII$^o_7$ BECOMES THE ROOT OF THE NEW-KEY VII$^o_7$.

Old key (C):   I   [VII$^o_7$ = VII$^o\,^4_3$ I$_6$ (V$^4_3$ I)]
(Major or minor)

New key (G♭ Major or minor)

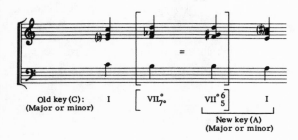

Old key (C):   I   [VII°₇   VII° 6/5   I
(Major or minor)

New key (A)
(Major or minor)

Used as shown above, the diminished seventh chord in each case provides the essential element for an enharmonic modulation similar in effect to the German Sixth enharmonic modulations discussed in Chapter 18. In both cases the modulating chord is a pivot chord that is notated differently in the two keys involved. VII°₇ functions as a dominant-quality chord whose root is the leading tone of the new key.

The diminished seventh chord may also function in a modulatory complex as a secondary diminished seventh chord in the new key. In this type of context the following modulatory progressions are possible:

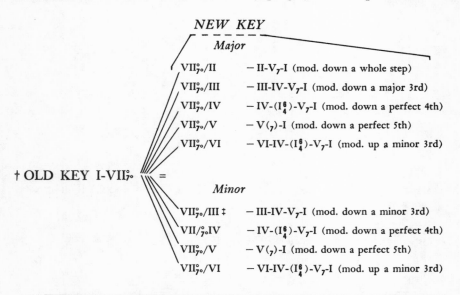

NEW KEY

Major

VII°₇/II	— II-V₇-I (mod. down a whole step)
VII°₇/III	— III-IV-V₇-I (mod. down a major 3rd)
VII°₇/IV	— IV-(I⁶₄)-V₇-I (mod. down a perfect 4th)
VII°₇/V	— V(₇)-I (mod. down a perfect 5th)
VII°₇/VI	— VI-IV-(I⁶₄)-V₇-I (mod. up a minor 3rd)

† OLD KEY I-VII°₇ =

Minor

VII°₇/III ‡	— III-IV-V₇-I (mod. down a minor 3rd)
VII/°₇IV	— IV-(I⁶₄)-V₇-I (mod. down a perfect 4th)
VII°₇/V	— V(₇)-I (mod. down a perfect 5th)
VII°₇/VI	— VI-IV-(I⁶₄)-V₇-I (mod. up a minor 3rd)

---

† This chord, and others in the above chart, are symbolized as root position chords. Remember, however, that any chord listed may be used in any inversion as well as in root position. The inversions producing the smoothest and most melodically-interesting part movement should be selected in each case.

‡ The major quality of the III chord (not the augmented quality) is generally used in minor keys.

Both of the German Sixth modulations given in Chapter 18 are adaptable to any combination of modalities. The only modification required for changing modes is that of lowering the third of the old-key I and/or lowering the third of the new-key I:

EXAMPLE 79. MODAL MODIFICATIONS OF EXAMPLE 68(B)—MODULATION TO A KEY A HALF STEP HIGHER, USING THE GERMAN SIXTH OF THE OLD KEY AS ENHARMONIC EQUIVALENT OF NEW-KEY V_7.

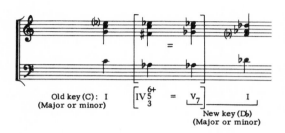

EXAMPLE 80. MODAL MODIFICATIONS OF EXAMPLE 70 (MODULATION TO A KEY A HALF STEP LOWER, USING V_7 OF THE OLD KEY AS ENHARMONIC EQUIVALENT OF NEW-KEY GERMAN SIXTH).

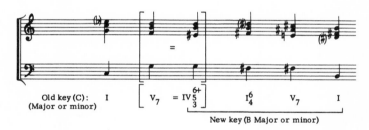

Pivot chord modulations are always practical between a major key and its closely-related minor keys—also between a minor key and its closely-related major keys. The closely-related keys to a particular key (major or minor) are as follows:

CLOSELY-RELATED KEYS

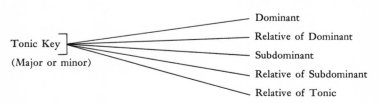

EXAMPLE 81. PIVOT MODULATION FROM A MAJOR KEY TO A CLOSELY-RELATED MINOR KEY.

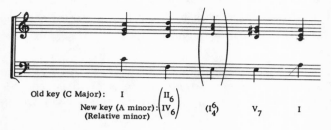

Old key (C Major):   I   (II₆)
New key (A minor): IV₆   (I⁶₄)   V₇   I
(Relative minor)

EXAMPLE 82. PIVOT MODULATION FROM A MINOR KEY TO A CLOSELY-RELATED MAJOR KEY.

Old key (C minor): I   (VI)
New key (E♭ Major): IV   V   (7)   I
(Relative Major)

Combinations of chromatic and enharmonic modulations can add color and surprise to a change of key. In the following example, old-key IV is converted chromatically to V₇ of the key a perfect fourth below, which chord in turn functions enharmonically as a German Sixth in the key a diminished fifth below the original tonic key.

EXAMPLE 83. COMBINED CHROMATIC AND ENHARMONIC MODULATION (ANY MODAL COMBINATION).

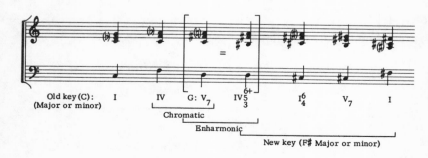

Old key (C):   I   IV   G: V₇   IV⁶⁺₅₃   I⁶₄   V₇   I
(Major or minor)
                                Chromatic
                                Enharmonic
                                        New key (F♯ Major or minor)

EXAMPLE 84. COMBINED CHROMATIC AND ENHARMONIC MODULATION (ANY MODAL COMBINATION).

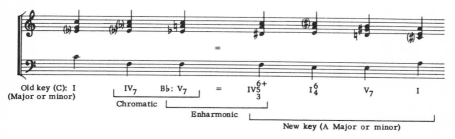

ASSIGNMENT NO. 19

A.   Select from the text of Chapter 19 a model for each of the following modulations, and play in all keys:

   (1)   A modulation using N_6 as a pivot to modulate from a minor key to a major key;
   (2)   A modulation using (major) old-key VII°_7 enharmonically as an inversion of (minor) new-key VII°_7;
   (3)   A modulation by pivot chord between two closely-related keys (one major, the other minor);
   (4)   A combined chromatic-enharmonic modulation from a minor key to another minor key.

B.   Connect each pair of excerpts by means of the indicated type of modulation. Use the appropriate type of texture for each example.

   1.   Use Example 72 (d) as a model.

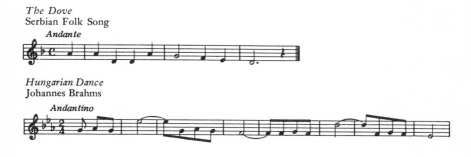

The Dove
Serbian Folk Song
Andante

Hungarian Dance
Johannes Brahms
Andantino

MODULATION   159

2. Use Example 81 as a model.

Allegretto
Franz Schubert

The Clock (excerpt)
Theodore Kullak

3. Use Example 83 as a model.

Hymn, *Old 107th*
Genevan Psalter

Hymn, *Urbs Beata*
George F. LeJeune

4. Use Example 75 as a model.

Joan Glover
Traditional English

Oh, I Pray You
Alessandro Scarlatti

5. Use Example 82 as a model.

Albumblatt
Ludwig Van Beethoven

Allegro
Wolfgang Amadeus Mozart

6. Use Example 76 as a model.

Hymn, *Aberystwyth*
Joseph Parry

Hymn, *Armageddon*
John Goss

7. Use Example 73 as a model.

O How Lovely
Robert Schumann

Song from *Susanna*
Georg Friedrich Händel

8. Use Example 77 as a model.

Trio
Franz Joseph Haydn

Preludio
Johann Sebastian Bach

Scherzando

Con moto

9. Use the following modulatory scheme:

Old key: I (minor)-$\left(\begin{array}{c}N_6\end{array}\right)$
New key (major) $\left(\begin{array}{c}V_6\end{array}\right)$-I-V$_5^6$-I

Hymn, *Cannons*
Georg Friedrich Händel

Hymn, *Bentley*
John Hullah

10. Use Example 84 as a model.

Might I Be
Giovanni Battista Pergolesi

Linda Amiga
Spanish Folk Song

11. Use the following modulatory scheme:

Old-key I-[VII$_7^0$ = New-key VII°$_2^4$]-I$_4^6$-V$_7$-I

The Doll's Burial
Peter Ilyitch Tschaikowsky

Romanze
Ludwig Van Beethoven

12. Use the following modulatory scheme:

Old-key: I-[VII$_7^0$ = New-key VII°$_7$/VI]-IV-V$_7$-I

Hymn, *Pentatone*
Henry W. Davies

Hymn, *St. Bride*
Samuel Howard

Sight Reading

THE DEVELOPMENT OF SIGHT-READING ABILITY IS A MATTER OF DIS-cipline. The essentials of this discipline are:

(1) Daily sight-reading practice (15 or 20 minutes);
(2) The availability of a large amount of easy to moderately difficult key-board music;
(3) Careful preliminary observation and analysis of every score before play-ing, *and during the act of playing;*
(4) The use, at every point, of materials considerably less difficult than the student's current repertoire.

It has been said that nine-tenths of a conductor's work must be done before he mounts the podium. To a certain extent this is also true of the sight reader, whose preliminary observations and analysis of the score are essential to proper performance.

There are several items of information *at the beginning of the score* that must be observed and understood before playing the music. These include:

Clefs;
Key signature;
Time signature;
Dynamic marking;
Tempo and/or metronome marking.

In the body of the score there occur items of information that—if observed and understood before playing begins—will contribute to ac-curacy and facility in performance:

Dynamic marks (accents, *crescendo, diminuendo,* etc.);
Repeat marks;
Phrasing (slurs, *staccato,* etc.);
Fingering;
D.C. and *D.S.* signs;
Changes in meter;
Changes in tempo;
Changes in clef.

Once a preliminary scanning of the score has been completed, and the information listed above has been noted, the performer is in a position to approach the additional problems of reading that occur during the actual performance of the music. These problems are analytical in nature, and have been discussed in relation to transposition in Chapters 12 through 14. Excellence in sight reading develops in proportion to the ability of the performer to read music as larger and larger complexes—melodic, harmonic, textural and formal. The achievement—by extended practice—of the ability to recognize musical structure in terms of harmony, counterpoint, texture and form is concomitant with the ability to sight-read well. To *know* what he is playing—in terms of musical structure—is the real objective of the musician who desires to achieve facility in reading at sight.

The following graded list of piano sight-reading materials ranges in degree of difficulty from very easy through easy, moderately easy and moderately difficult; textures vary from two-part through three- and four-part; there are linear, chordal and figured textures in a variety of commonly-used keys and meters. It is suggested that the student supplement these materials with additional music from other sources; or he may prefer to develop his own complete list of progressive sight-reading materials. (It is important that music used for sight reading be at least two grades easier than that of his current repertoire.) After the preliminary observations of the score have been carefully made, each piece should be read three times at a comfortable tempo, with the performer "reading ahead" —not note by note—but in terms of structural complexes—the larger the better.

GRADED LIST OF SIGHT-READING MATERIALS

I. ROYAL CONSERVATORY OF TORONTO— *PIANO BOOK I* (Summy-Birchard)

(1) *Study No. 5,* p. 26
(2) *Study No. 2,* p. 24

V. MIROVITCH, *COMMAND OF THE KEYBOARD*, Vol. I (Presser)

(43) *Etude in F* (Ricci), p. 25
(44) *Etude in B♭* (Ricci), p. 24
(45) *Little Serenade* (Ricci), p. 23
(46) *Graceful Dance* (Ricci), p. 21
(47) *Etude in A minor* (Ricci), p. 26
(48) *March* (Leopold Mozart), p. 14
(49) *Rhythm* (Ricci), p. 12
(50) *Etude* (Seiffert), p. 13
(51) *Staccato* (Ricci), p. 10
(52) *Etude* (Hassler), p. 11

VI. MIROVITCH, *COMMAND OF THE KEYBOARD*, Vol. II (Presser)

(53) *Prelude* (Heller), p. 15
(54) *Etude* (Bertini), p. 7
(55) *The Cuckoo* (Gnessin), p. 8
(56) *Vivace* (Hassler), p. 6
(57) *March* (Leopold Mozart), p. 5
(58) *Quick March* (Kossenko), p. 10

VII. *SELECTED SONATINAS*, Vol. II [Podolsky, editor] (Belwin)

(59) *Sonatina*—Complete (Biehl), p. 6
(60) *Allegro* (Haydn), p. 105
(61) *Sonatina*—Last movement (Clementi), p. 42
(62) *Sonatina*—Last movement (Clementi), p. 38
(63) *Sonatina*—First movement (Clementi), p. 36
(64) *Sonatina*—First movement (Clementi), p. 40
(65) *Sonatina*—Second movement (Clementi), p. 46

VIII. TSCHAIKOWSKY, *ALBUM FOR THE YOUNG* (Schirmer)

(66) *The Sick Doll*, p. 8
(67) *The Doll's Burial*, p. 9
(68) *Russian Song*, p. 14
(69) *Old French Song*, p. 19
(70) *Italian Song*, p. 18
(71) *In Church*, p. 31

IX. *SELECTED PIANO SOLOS BY ROMANTIC COMPOSERS*, Vol. I (Schirmer)

(72) *Prayer* (Gurlitt), p. 1
(73) *Chorale* (Gurlitt), p. 3
(74) *Distant Bells* (Streabogg), p. 4

(75) *March of the Tin Soldiers* (Gurlitt), p. 14
(76) *Serious Moments* (Gurlitt), p. 16
(77) *Morning Prayer* (Tschaikowsky), p. 35
(78) *Strolling Musicians* (Rebikov), p. 40
(79) *Trumpeter's Serenade* (Spindler), p. 44
(80) *The Clock* (Kullak), p. 29
(81) *Waltz* (Gurlitt), p. 10

X. REINHOLD, *MINIATURES* (Schirmer)

(82) *At School*, p. 12
(83) *Fairy Tale*, p. 4
(84) *Silhouette*, p. 14
(85) *Gypsy Song*, p. 15
(86) *Arietta*, p. 16
(87) *Slumber Song*, p. 17
(88) *Nocturne*, p. 21
(89) *Melancholy*, p. 23

ADDITIONAL COLLECTIONS OF PIECES FOR SIGHT READING (MORE ADVANCED)

Bauer, *Eight Diversions from a Composer's Notebook* (Chappell)
Podolsky, *Musical Finds from the 17th and 18th Centuries* (Summy-Birchard)
Piano Literature of the 17th, 18th and 19th Centuries, Vol. II (Summy-Birchard)
Scher, *Fifteen Descriptive Miniatures* (Ditson)
Agay, *Panorama of Easy Pieces by Modern Masters* (Presser)
Levine, *Themes from the Great Ballets* (Presser)
Kullak, *Scenes from Childhood* (Schirmer)
Selected Piano Pieces by Romantic Composers, Vol. II (Schirmer)
Mendelssohn, *Songs Without Words* (Schirmer)

EASY HYMNS FOR SIGHT READING

The following forty hymns are in easy keys, and contain a minimum of embellishment, moving for the most part in quarter notes and half notes. They are all to be found in *Christian Hymns* (North River Press), and the page numbers given refer to this publication. However, most of these hymns, and many others of like degree of difficulty, can be found in other hymnals (Episcopal, Lutheran, Methodist, Baptist, Presbyterian, etc.). They can be located by means of the indices by title.

NUMBER	TUNE	KEY	PAGE
1	Rathbun	C	106
2	Ombersley	C	250
3	Deus Tuorum Militum	C	381
4	St. Anne	C	198
5	St. Petersburg	C	118
6	Colchester	C	387
7	Penitence	C	344
8	Tallis' Canon	G	10
9	Sandon	G	65
10	Ilfracomb	G	107
11	Italian Hymn	G	143
12	St. Catherine	G	156
13	Stephanos	G	162
14	Arlington	G	207
15	St. Agnes	G	268
16	Old 134th (St. Michael)	G	191
17	Hursley	F	16
18	Dennis	F	55
19	Praetorius	F	61
20	Hamburg	F	108
21	Martyn	F	177
22	Quam Delecta	F	202
23	St. Flavian	F	210
24	Near The Cross	F	254
25	Trentham	F	169
26	Gordon	F	260
27	Herongate	D	81
28	Darwall	D	130
29	Sweet Hour	D	313
30	Swabia	D	206
31	Truro	D	390
32	Samuel	D	478
33	Monsell	B♭	44
34	Wareham	B♭	160
35	Ernan	B♭	297
36	Webb	B♭	337
37	Germany	B♭	393
38	Festal Song	B♭	300
39	Arthur's Seat	B♭	335
40	Bethlehem	B♭	376

INDEX